Paul, the apostle, urges ~~pattern of this world, but be transformed by the renewing of your mind.' In his book *The Lord's Day*, Dr. Pipa courageously and accurately identifies a major issue of lifestyle on which the majority of Christians in this century have caved in to the pattern of this world. Even the best taught Christians have abandoned the heritage of the Protestant Reformation in this matter; but worse still they have disobeyed Biblical standards which guided saints of former ages.

This book is clearly under-girded by thorough exegesis, wise scholarship and a broad knowledge of the church history on the subject of the Sabbath. Yet it is written with the plainness and warmth of pastoral experience which will benefit the youngest Christian. Every believer will find an abundance of practical direction for keeping the Lord's Day in our modern world.

If the Church of Christ does not heed the principles of God's Word on the issue addressed in this book, she will be overwhelmed by 'the pattern of this world' and more seriously weakened. The Sabbath is one of God's appointed means for 'renewing' the Christian mind.

Walter J. Chantry
Pastor, Grace Baptist Church
Carlisle, Pennsylvania

Professor Pipa has written a splendid book on the Lord's Day as the Christian Sabbath. It combines careful and convincing examination of the Bible with helpful, pastoral application. The book breathes the spirit of the gospel and truly shows the delightful character of God's provision of a day of worship and rest for His people. The church has needed this book. Use your Sunday afternoons to read it!

W. Robert Godfrey
Westminster West Theological Seminary
Escandido, California

Dr. Joseph A. Pipa is Director of Advanced Studies at Westminster Theological Seminary in California. He directs the Doctor of Ministry program in Preaching and also teaches Systematic, Historical and Practical Theology at the Master's level. A graduate of Belhaven College and Reformed Theological Seminary in Jackson, Mississippi, he received a Ph.D. from Westminster Theological Seminary in Philadelphia, Pennsylvania. He is the author of *Root and Branch*, a study of the person and work of Christ (also published by Christian Focus).

THE
LORD'S DAY

Joseph A. Pipa

Christian Focus

© Joseph A. Pipa
ISBN 1 85792 201 8

Published in 1997
by
Christian Focus Publications, Geanies House, Fearn,
Ross-shire, IV20 1TW, Great Britain.

Cover design by Paz Design, 1320 Edgewater Road,
Suite 200, Salem, Oregon 97305, USA

Printed in Great Britain by
The Guernsey Press Co Ltd, Vale, Guernsey, Channel Islands

CONTENTS

DEDICATION

I dedicate this book to two men who in my youth taught me about the Christian Sabbath and to a young lady who represents the generation after me. The men are my pastor while in High School, Mr. Donald Patterson, who first taught me about the importance of the Lord's Day, and Dr. Morton Smith, my theological mentor, who showed me the biblical basis for the Christian Sabbath. The young lady is my daughter, Sara Elizabeth Pipa, who from her earliest days has loved the Sabbath and called it a delight (Psalm 78:1-8).

A DAY FOR BLESSING

Once there was a great king who built a splendid city. In the middle of the city, the king designed a delightful park which was laid out with ponds, fountains and springs, magnificent trees from all over the world, gorgeous aromatic plants, inviting stretches of lawn, pathways and benches where people and families might walk and sit together, and a spacious amphitheatre for public meetings. Weekly the king met with his subjects in the park. His people delighted in the time with him and one another.

One day the king had to go away. In his absence the rulers he left in charge began to let the park run down. Although they still held civic events at the amphitheatre, these rulers had little interest in the park. They did not truly have in mind the king's interests. Soon the park was overrun with weeds, the trees were not pruned, the exotic plants died, and the pools of water stagnated. The park was in ruins.

After a time a new group of rulers came into authority in the city. They were genuinely concerned about the park and began to restore it to its former beauty. They pulled out all the weeds, replanted all the gardens, pruned the trees, repaired the pathways and the benches, and opened the streams so that fresh water again flowed through the park. These rulers, however, were fearful that the park once again would fall into disrepair. In order to protect the park they made it a memorial to the king, rather like a museum. They continued to hold meetings at the amphitheatre, but they put a fence around the park's border and along the pathways so people could look at the beautiful sites in the park, but could not actually use it.

Then one day, quite unexpectedly, the king's son came to the city. One of the first things that he did was to tear down the fence. He exclaimed to the rulers, 'Enough of this! This park was built for the people of the city to remember my father and enjoy, but you have kept them out of the park.' So after removing all of the fences, he invited the people to come and meet with him and one another in the park.

Because the king and his son are still occupied throughout their great kingdom, they have appointed leaders in the city. Regrettably, of late these leaders once again have allowed the park to become unkempt and trampled down. Again, weeds overrun it, the trees are not pruned, and the ponds have become stagnant. Because it has lost much of its charming beauty, people no longer come to it. Admittedly they have kept the amphitheatre in good repair and continue public meetings, but increasingly the people are losing interest. The park is so unattractive that they see no need to go there at all.

Recently, developers, seeing the land unused, have begun seeking to put up an amusement park. The Historical Society is opposing them, wanting instead to restore the park and preserve it for the sake of tradition. But there is a third group who wants to restore it to its original purposes. To make matters more confusing, all parties are claiming to act on behalf of the interests of the king and his son. Meanwhile, as you might imagine, the king's subjects are thoroughly confused.

The story of the park is a parable of the controversy over the use of the Lord's day. I represent those who want to see the park restored to its original purposes. Therefore, the object of this book is to make a biblical case for Sunday as the Christian Sabbath and to answer the objections of those who think the Sabbath ordinance is a Mosaic institution that has been fulfilled in Christ. All agree that the Church needs a day for corporate worship. While some maintain that the Church is free to establish any day of the week and others insist that Christ has appointed the first day of the week for the Church to worship, they agree that people are free to use the remainder of the day as they please. Others would like to see the day restored to its traditional role, but seem to have lost sight of its original purpose. I believe that we should keep the day according to God's law, for the purpose of delighting in and enjoying Him. The day is to be a day of blessing as the hymnwriter says:

> O day of rest and gladness,
>   O day of joy and light,
> O balm of care and sadness,
>   Most beautiful, most bright.

This book is an attempt at an exegetical, doctrinal and historical examination of the Sabbath day as a Christian institution. Furthermore, convinced of its practical beauty and utility, I offer four chapters on the profitable use of the day.

I have written the book as a popular exposition of the Christian Sabbath. Although I interact with the various arguments and objections against the idea of the Christian Sabbath in the body of the book, I use the footnotes to give more detailed information on various positions and writers for those who want to do a more critical study.

I would like to thank those who have helped in the preparation of this book. Special thanks to Mrs. Caroline

Brown for her careful reading and stylistic suggestions and to my colleague and friend Dr. S.M. Baugh for his helpful input. I also would like to thank Mr. Howard Griffith and Mrs. Alaine Hofland for their encouragement and helpful insights. Then thanks to all of those who helped with typing: Mrs. Phyllis Wilson, my secretary; Mrs. Jackie Vanden Bos; Mrs. Jill Klein; and Mrs. Liz Timmermans. I would also like to thank the Trustees of Westminster Seminary in California for granting me a sabbatical so that I might complete this book. Last of all, but by no means least, I would acknowledge the encouragement and suggestions of my wonderful wife, 'Sissy', whom our God has given me as a 'helper corresponding to my needs'.

1

THE GREAT PURPOSE
(Isaiah 58:13,14)

The parable of the park illustrates the great controversy swirling around Sunday and Sabbath observance. Much as environmentalists and developers square off to fight over a parcel of land, sabbatarians and anti-sabbatarians are embroiled in controversy over the proper use of Sunday. Often such controversy results in our losing sight of the beauties and pleasures of the day, so that the Lord's day is marred and disfigured much as it was in the days of the Pharisees.

Historically, the purpose of sabbatarianism was not to create a legalistic entanglement that stifles people, but to free the people of God for the wonderful privilege of worshipping God and enjoying Him. The Sabbath and its observance really is like a park – not only to be protected but also to be used and enjoyed according to God's purpose. Therefore, we shall begin this study by examining the purpose of the Sabbath.

That purpose is spelled out in the wonderful promise found in Isaiah 58:13,14. In this chapter the prophet exposes the lifeless formalism in the worship of God's people. He rebukes them for clinging to sin while going through the motions of worship. As an antidote to this formalism he sets before them the great privilege of the Sabbath and the blessings of God that attend it, saying that the God of the covenant solemnly promises great spiritual blessings to those

11

who keep the Sabbath day holy: 'Then you will take delight in the LORD and I will make you ride on the heights of the earth, and I will feed you with the heritage of Jacob your father.' I do not know three more wonderful things promised in all the Bible than what God pledges here.

God's promises to those who keep the Sabbath
First, He promises unsurpassed communion with God, '[Y]ou will take delight in the LORD.' The word 'delight' means 'exquisite pleasure'. To take exquisite pleasure in the Lord is to be overwhelmed by His beauty and glory that are revealed in His attributes and work. To delight in God is to enjoy special communion and fellowship with Him, responding with gratitude and delight as He manifests His love to you. This communion is captured by the emblem of a luxuriant garden adorned with beautiful foliage where God meets with you (Song of Songs 4:16). Do any of us love and enjoy God as much as we should? God designed the Sabbath as a means of our enjoying Him through special communion with Him. On the Sabbath you will find exquisite pleasure in God.

But there is more. He adds, 'And I will make you ride on the heights of the earth.' He borrows this language of victory from Deuteronomy 32:12–13 and 33:29. In these verses God promises Israel great victory over her enemies. Earlier, Isaiah uses this language to promise the people victory over their enemies (Isa. 33:16). Their return from exile is a picture of the victory promised in the New Covenant. In the New Testament God promises us victory as well: in Christ we are more than conquerors (Rom. 8:37); we shall have victory over Satan and sin. According to Isaiah 58:14, God promises this victory to those who keep His day holy. Sabbath-keeping is a means of grace[1] that will help you die to sin and grow in holiness.

Is it not possible that one reason for the spiritual weakness of the church is her failure to honour God on the Lord's day? Is it not possible that one reason our churches are not more effective in reaching the lost is because we are not practising the Sabbath-keeping that brings us victory? Could this be true of us as individuals as well? Is it not possible that you continue to fall under the dominion of some particular sin because you have refused to sanctify God's day in your heart? We lack victory because we have failed to recognize and utilize one of the God-given means of victory, while those who keep the Sabbath have victory.

Moreover, in addition to the promises of exquisite pleasure in the Lord and victory over our enemies, He promises a practical enjoyment of the benefits of our salvation, 'I will feed you with the heritage of Jacob your father.' To 'feed on an inheritance' is to enjoy its benefits. God promises Israel that they will enjoy again the inheritance promised to Abraham, Isaac, and Jacob (Psalm 105:10–11). The possession of the land was a symbol of the inheritance of God's covenant people. Not only will He restore their land, but also He will give a prosperity in which they will fully enjoy all the benefits of their possession (Psalm 144:12–15).

How does this promise apply to us? Our inheritance includes the benefits of salvation: adoption, assurance of salvation, boldness in prayer, confidence. This promise means

---

1. The 'means of grace' are those things appointed by God to help us grow as Christians. The Larger Catechism defines means of grace as 'The outward and ordinary means whereby Christ communicates to His church the benefits of His mediation...' In Chapter 4 we will examine in more detail how the Sabbath aids in our sanctification.

we will revel in our privileges as children of God. These benefits are not merely a list of privileges to memorize; they are spiritual pleasures to be enjoyed – the everyday practical participation in your privileges as a child of God.

Notice as well the remarkable certainty of the promise, 'For the mouth of the LORD has spoken.' Isaiah often uses this phrase to highlight the certainty of specific promises; particularly promises that have to do with the Messiah and the remission of sin. Take, for example, Isaiah 1:18-20. After promising remission of sins to those who repent, but threatening judgment on those who refuse God's offer, the prophet concludes, 'Truly, the mouth of the LORD has spoken it.' Or consider Isaiah 25:8: 'He will swallow up death for all time, and the LORD will wipe tears away from all faces, and He will remove the reproach of His people from all the earth; for the LORD has spoken' (cf. 40:5).

Do you see what God is doing? By the declaration, 'for the mouth of the LORD has spoken,' He guarantees the promise. Could any better guarantee be given? The Lord God puts it all on the line. He says, 'I the Lord God who cannot lie, I promise that if you keep my Sabbath and delight in it, you will delight in me, gain spiritual victory and enjoy your inheritance.'

Does the promise still apply?

Some object, 'God gave this promise to Israel as His Old Testament people. Is it appropriate for us to claim this promise today?' We do not use this line of reasoning with the wonderful things the Old Testament says about marriage or the place of our children in the Covenant. Why use it here? The moral and spiritual commands, as well as many of the Old Testament promises, apply to us, and we may not dismiss a threat or promise simply because it is found in the Old Testament.

Among other things, we consider the context of the promise when seeking to determine how it applies. This entire section of Isaiah refers ultimately to Jesus Christ and the New Covenant people. The section begins with the famous promise of the suffering servant in chapter 53. In chapter 54:1-3 the prophet assures the church of its world-wide outreach:

> Shout for joy, O barren one,
> you who have borne no *child*;
> Break forth into joyful shouting and cry aloud,
>   you who have not travailed;
> For the sons of the desolate one will be more numerous
> Than the sons of the married woman.
> Enlarge the place of your tent;
> Stretch out the curtains of your dwelling, spare not;
> Lengthen your cords,
> And strengthen your pegs.
> For you will spread abroad to the right and the left.
> And your descendants will possess nations,
> And they will resettle the desolate cities.

In chapter 55:1 he calls sinners to repentance:

> Ho, everyone who thirsts, come to the waters;
> And you who have no money, come buy and eat.
> Come buy wine and milk
> Without money and without cost.

All of this material refers to the New Testament era.

In chapter 56 God begins to relate the Sabbath to the New Testament people. He says in 56:2-5:

> How blessed is the man who does this
> and the son of man who takes hold of it,
> who keeps from profaning the Sabbath,
> and keeps his hand from doing any evil.
> Let not the foreigner who has joined himself to the LORD say,
> 'The LORD will surely separate me from His people.'
> Neither let the eunuch say, 'Behold I am a dry tree.'
> For thus says the LORD,
> 'To the eunuchs who keep My Sabbaths,
> And choose what pleases Me,
> And hold fast My covenant,
> To them I will give in My house and within My walls a memorial.

How do we know that this applies to the New Testament era? Because only in the gospel era may a eunuch enjoy the privileges promised here. In Deuteronomy 23:1, God declares that a eunuch may not enter the house of the Lord. Here, anticipating the reign of the Christ, God promises the eunuch that he shall receive a great memorial name in the house of the Lord.[2] The prophet is relating Sabbath-keeping to the days of the New Covenant and the glories of the church of the Lord Jesus Christ.

We may conclude, therefore, that the promise of Isaiah 58:13–14 is for the New Testament church. Surely every Christian longs for the things promised: intimate communion with God, spiritual victory, and practical enjoyment of his privileges.

The conditions of the promise
But in order to receive these promises, you must meet the conditions spelled out in verse 13:

---

2. Edward J. Young, *The Book of Isaiah*, 3 vols. (Grand Rapids: Eerdmans, 1974), III, 390, 391.

> If because of the Sabbath, you turn your foot
> From doing your *own* pleasure on My holy day,
> And call the Sabbath a delight, the holy *day* of the LORD
>   honorable,
> And shall honor it, desisting from your *own* ways,
> From seeking your *own* pleasure,
> And speaking *your own* word, ...

In order to enjoy the promise you must have a proper regard for the Sabbath. First, Isaiah states the condition negatively, 'If because of the Sabbath you turn your foot from doing your own pleasure on My holy day.' Because the Sabbath is the holy day of the Lord you are not to profane it.

Anticipating the language of the New Testament (that Jesus is Lord of the Sabbath, Matthew 12:8;[3] and that the New Testament Sabbath is called the Lord's day, Revelation 1:10[4]), Isaiah refers to the Sabbath as God's 'holy day' and 'the holy day of the Lord'. The Sabbath is considered a holy day because God Himself sanctified it. In Genesis 2:2-3 we read: 'And by the seventh day God completed His work which He had done; and He rested on the seventh day from all His work which He had done. Then God blessed the seventh day and sanctified it, because in it He rested from all His work which God had created and made.' After God had completed His work of creation in six days, He set apart the seventh day to be holy.

What does it mean that God makes a day holy? I will examine this concept more fully in Chapter 2, but note that when God sanctified something He set it aside from its everyday common use so that it might be used exclusively in worship. Thus in the Old Testament He sanctified places,

---

3. See chapter 5. 4. See chapter 8.

garments, altars and other such things that they might be
dedicated to His worship. Therefore, when God makes a day
holy, He separates it from its normal everyday uses to the
exclusive purposes of worship. When He sets aside the
Sabbath day for worship, even those things legitimately done
on other days of the week are prohibited, because He has
designated that day for worship.

How does one profane the Sabbath? By doing his own
pleasure on it. This word 'pleasure' is used throughout the
Old Testament to describe those things in which one delights
(Ps. 1:2; Isa. 44:28; 46:10; 58:3; Ecc. 3:1,17; 8:6). In our
modern idiom we could paraphrase it 'doing your own thing';
'Doing your pleasure' refers to those things you enjoy doing
or must do the other six days: business, work, play, or
whatever. When you do these things on God's holy day you
desecrate it. You trample it underfoot like children who run
over flower beds in a park. If you want to enjoy the promise
of God, you must not profane the day by doing your own
pleasure.

God does not forbid our work or pleasure on the Sabbath
because He is opposed to pleasure. Rather, He is calling us
to turn aside from lesser pleasures in order to seek the greater
pleasures He has in store for us in the day. Thus the prophet
continues by telling us what to do. Positively, we are to
honour and revere the day: 'call the Sabbath a delight, the
holy day of the LORD, honorable.' Not only are we to refrain
from profaning the day, but also we must honour it and delight
in it as God's holy day.

We are to consider the Sabbath a delight. The word
'delight' is a form of the word used in verse 14, 'to delight
in God.' As we noted above, the word means 'to take exquisite
pleasure'. As we delight in beloved people or beautiful

things, so we are to delight in the spiritual exercises of the day. We are to take great pleasure in worship, fellowship, and Christian service. With this command Isaiah begins to attack the formalism alluded to above. Proper worship and Sabbath-keeping spring from an exuberant delight in the spiritual exercises of the day.

Furthermore, we delight in the day as we honour it. Since God has set it aside, we are to honour the day as special, the holy day of the Lord. This is what God means in the fourth commandment when He says, 'Remember the Sabbath day, to keep it holy.'[5] We remember the Sabbath day by taking exquisite delight in that day and calling it honourable.

'If this is the case,' you ask, 'how do I honour it?' You honour the day by doing three things: 'desisting from your own ways, from seeking your own pleasure, and speaking your own word' (Isa. 58:13).

First, you are not to do your regular work: 'desisting from your own ways.' You are to cease doing your business – the affairs and responsibilities of everyday living. The word translated 'ways' is a general term that applies to any number of activities. Some suggest that this word does not refer to business and work, but rather the way of sin. They point out that Isaiah uses the term in reference to the way of sin in Isaiah 53:6: 'All of us like sheep have gone astray, each of us has turned to his own way' (cf. Prov. 1:31; Isa. 66:3).

Although the phrase 'your ways' may at times refer to sinful acts, in other places it refers broadly to the activities of life: Proverbs 3:6, 'In all your ways acknowledge Him and He will make your paths straight' (cf. Prov. 23:26; 31:3; Isa. 45:13). In the immediate context Isaiah uses the phrase

---

5. See Chapter 3.

'My ways' to refer to God's will (Isa. 58:2). The phrase, therefore, is neutral. One must determine from the context whether it is an evil way, the way of God, or the ways of our regular business, duty and pleasure. Since Isaiah 58:13 is the condition of the special promise in verse 14 and includes the command to honour the Sabbath, the context suggests the interpretation 'the activities of our business and pleasure'. It is a given that one may not do sinful things on the Sabbath, but God is saying here that those activities that are permissible the other six days become sinful when done on the Sabbath. The prophet is applying the prohibition of the fourth commandment, that we are not to work nor are we to work others. God has given us six days to do our business; the seventh belongs to Him. Thus, besides works of necessity (Matt. 12:1-8)[6] or mercy (Matt. 12:9-14)[7] we are not to pursue business on the Lord's day.

This means you should not be going into the office or working in the store on Sunday. You ought not to be doing homework or unnecessary housework. Nor should you cause others to work, so you should avoid eating out, going to the grocery store or the mall, or travelling extensively for business. One increasingly frequent violation is Christian business people and pastors who fly on Sundays, either to be home for work by Monday morning or ready to begin business in some other city. Is such travel using the day for God's purposes?[8]

Second, you are not to use Sunday for play or amusement, 'seeking your own pleasure.'[9] The word 'pleasure' is the

---

6. See Chapter 5.
7. See Chapter 6.
8. For a discussion of the positive use of the day see chapters10-12.
9. Moshe Weinfeld argues that the phrases 'seeking your own pleasure and speaking your own word' refers to business transactions, 'Weinfeld: Counsel of

same word used in the first clause of the verse when God says, 'Turn your foot from doing your own pleasure on My holy day.' Note the relation between this stipulation and the promise: if you delight in the spiritual exercises of the day and do not seek your own pleasure, you will take great pleasure in God. You are not to pursue your own pleasure in playing or recreation. Rather, you are to discover the peculiar treasure of the Sabbath, to take exquisite delight in what it offers. Thus we profane the day by watching television, going to movies or ball games, or using the day for sports.

God is not opposed to fun properly used. Moderate recreation on the other six days is a gift of God. The Sabbath, though, is to be devoted to the peculiar spiritual pleasures of worship and service. God frees us from pursuing lesser pleasures that we might pursue greater and more noble things. We are to look at the Lord's day like a spiritual vacation. I eagerly anticipate a vacation as a time to forget about job pressures and enjoy my family. God gives us a weekly vacation that we may turn away from mundane, everyday activities and enjoy Him.

This, though, should not be interpreted as a prohibition of

---

the 'Elders', in *MAARAV, A Journal for the Study of the Northwest Semitic Languages and Literatures* (Santa Monica: Western Academic Press, Vol III, No.1, January 1982) 43-45. For the interpretation I take see Young, III, 427, 'There is no need to restrict these phrases to matters of business. The "way" is a course of conduct and refers to all courses and actions that men choose in preference to the commands of God. These courses and actions may be right and legitimate on other days, but when they obtrude in the place of that delight, which is to find expression in the observance of the Sabbath, they are to be refrained from. Secondly, *not finding thy pleasure* also refers to one's own pleasure in distinction from what pleases God; and the third expression, *speaking words* (the noun is best understood as collective), probably refers to idle and vain talk, in which God is forgotten or ignored. What is mentioned tends to draw the heart away from God to the consideration of one's own occupations. This is wrong conduct on the holy Sabbath.'

all physical activity. Your children will need some physical activity. In Chapter 11 I will give a number suggestions for structuring the day for our children. Adults, as well, might need some type of physical activity in order to be alert for evening worship.

Nor is God opposed to rest. Many wrongly interpret the requirement of Shorter Catechism 'spending the whole time in the public and private exercises of God's worship, except so much as is to be taken up in the works of necessity and mercy'[10] to prohibit resting. True, the rest of this day is not a rest of idleness or recreation. It is a rest that enables us to enjoy the purposes of the day and equips us to serve God the other six days. Moderate physical rest, however, may be a 'work of necessity' to enable one to keep the Sabbath properly.

Third, we ought to avoid unnecessary conversation about work and recreations: 'cease speaking your own word.' We are not to converse about our work, pleasures and hobbies, but rather we are to set our minds on the things of the Lord. This does not rule out conversation with Christian friends about work or family affairs. In order to have true fellowship we need to know what is going on in each others' lives. But God wants us to avoid needless conversation about our recreation and work.

The Westminster Shorter Catechism gives an apt summary of the requirement of Isaiah 58:13:

What is forbidden in the fourth commandment?
The fourth commandment forbiddeth the omission or careless performance of the duties required and the profaning the day by idleness or doing that which is in itself sinful or by

---

10. *Westminster Shorter Catechism* 60.

unnecessary thoughts words or works about our worldly
employments or recreations.[11]

Too often we stop with the negative and the day is accented
by the 'do nots.' God, however, does not want you to define
the day by what you may not do, but rather by what you may
do. Why does God want you to cease from doing your own
business? Why does God tell you to stop pursuing your own
pleasure and speaking your own words? So that you may
pursue His business, that you may seek the pleasures of His
word and work, and that you may delight in His worship and
word.

How then should you spend the day? *The Shorter
Catechism*'s question 60 helps us:

> The Sabbath is to be sanctified by a holy resting all that day,
> even from such worldly employments and recreations as are
> lawful on other days, and spending the whole time in the public
> and private exercises of God's worship.[12]

All true Sabbath-keeping begins by our actively resting in
God alone for our salvation. Without actively focusing on
Christ and living in dependence on Him there is no true
Sabbath-keeping. Moreover as we turn aside from our work
and pleasure, we are freed to worship Him corporately with
His people, privately in our homes. We have time to serve
Him by speaking His word, by going to the nursing home, by
visiting the sick and the shut-in, by witnessing and passing
out tracts, by teaching and preaching His word. We have the
luxury of having people into our homes that we may enjoy
their fellowship and minister to them.

---

11. *Ibid.* 61.
12. Chapters 9-11 will deal with suggestions on keeping the Sabbath and using it
for God's glory.

The Sabbath day is a great gift that God has given to us so that we might have the time for these pleasures. God wants us to focus on the gift of the day.

Sabbath observance has been the practice and conviction of most Christians from the Reformation until fifty to seventy-five years ago. It remains on paper a commitment of most Presbyterian and Reformed denominations. For example, my denomination, The Presbyterian Church in America, states in its *Directory of Worship*:

> Therefore it is requisite that there be a holy resting all the day from unnecessary labors, and of abstaining from those recreations which may be lawful on other days, and also, as much as possible, from worldly thought and conversation. Let the time not used for public worship be spent in prayer, devotional reading, and especially in the study of the Scriptures, meditation, catechizing, religious conversation, singing of psalms, hymns, or spiritual songs, visiting the sick, relieving the poor, teaching the ignorant, holy resting, and in performing such like duties with piety, charity, and mercy.

God promises that He will cause you to delight in Him, to have spiritual victory, and to enjoy the benefits of the gospel. Is there any one who enjoys the grace of the gospel and the power of the Holy Spirit who does not want what God promises here? God solemnly swears, 'If you want to delight in Me, if you want this exquisite pleasure and victory, stop profaning My day; rather call it a delight. Honour it by ceasing from your own ways, from your own pleasures, from speaking your own words.'

As we further examine the Bible's teaching, may the Lord give us all hearts to understand and wills to respond.

2

THE ORIGINAL INTENT
(Genesis 2:1-3)

As noted, a great controversy is swirling on the issue of the Christian Sabbath. Should Sunday be considered the Sabbath? Does the Bible require the Christian to observe one day in seven, or are all days equal? Is the appointment of Sunday for worship merely a matter of the church's need to agree on a day for worship? Growing numbers of people are repudiating the idea that Sunday is the Christian Sabbath.[1]

Although there has always been controversy surrounding the application of the Sabbath to the Lord's day, until recently a large majority of Christians maintained that both church and society were under a moral obligation to refrain from work and public recreation on Sunday, and that Christians should observe the day according to the Fourth Commandment.

Which view is correct? What should we do? Should we decide for contemporary practice or for the historical practice of the church? Is the park to be restored back to its purpose and uses as described in Isaiah 58:13-14, or is it to be levelled? Obviously we have the spiritual needs addressed by Sabbath observance. If it was a means of grace once, why not now? But can we say more? Does the Bible give a clear answer? The answer lies in rediscovering the king's intent in designing the park. We shall look at Genesis 2:1-3 to discover God's intention for the Sabbath and mankind.

---

1. For contemporary works against sabbatarianism see D.A. Carson, ed., *From Sabbath to Lord's Day* (Grand Rapids: Zondervan, 1982) and Paul K. Jewett, *The Lord's Day* (Grand Rapids: Eerdmans, 1972).

Ceremonial laws and permanent laws

All concede that the Fourth Commandment requires a careful observance of the Sabbath. The question is whether this commandment was a temporary ceremonial law or a permanent moral law. In the Bible there are temporary laws called positive laws and also permanent laws called moral laws.

A positive law is a commandment of God that is not morally necessary. (By this I mean the thing commanded in and of itself is not inherently right or wrong.) God requires or forbids certain things for the immediate and temporary needs of His people and their relationship to Him. Such laws are binding only on the person or nation to whom they were given. For example, the prohibition to Adam and Eve not to eat of the fruit of the tree of the knowledge of good and evil was a positive law. There was nothing uniquely or inherently holy about eating or not eating, rather the prohibition was the means which God chose to test their willingness to obey Him (Gen. 2:16-17). The ceremonial laws of the Mosaic Covenant are also examples of positive law. For example, there is nothing inherently evil about eating pork. In order to teach His people His sovereignty over all of life, even what they ate, God declared pork unclean Now, under the New Covenant, God has repealed the food laws and teaches His people to eat and drink what was previously forbidden to His glory (1 Cor. 10:31; 1 Tim. 4:3-5).

A moral law, on the other hand, is a commandment that reflects the moral nature of God and our relation to Him and one another. These laws are absolutely necessary for the spiritual well-being of the image-bearer of God. Moral laws are permanently binding on all people. Murder is wrong, not only because God's Word prohibits it, but also because it is inherently evil. Thus, 'You shall not commit murder' is a permanently binding obligation on all people in all ages.

Although there are temporary aspects involved in Old Testament Sabbath observance (more about this below), the principle of a special day devoted to the worship and service of God is a perpetually binding moral obligation. *The Westminster Confession of Faith* sets this out clearly:

> As it is of the law of nature, that, in general, a due proportion of time be set apart for the worship of God; so, in His word, by a positive, moral, and perpetual commandment, binding all men in all ages, He hath particularly appointed one day in seven for a Sabbath, to be kept holy unto Him; which, from the beginning of the world to the resurrection of Christ, was the last day of the week; and, from the resurrection of Christ, was changed into the first day of the week, which in Scripture is called the Lord's day, and is to be continued to the end of the world, as the Christian Sabbath.[2]

The conviction that Sabbath observance is a perpetually binding obligation is based in part on God's institution of the Sabbath in Genesis 2:1-3. Along with work (Gen. 1:24; 2:15) and marriage (Gen. 2:18-25), God instituted the Sabbath to govern the lives of all mankind. Just as the ordinances of work and marriage are permanent, so is the ordinance of the Sabbath.[3]

In Genesis 1 Moses has recorded the creative work of God on the first six days of history. Genesis 2, building on this theology of creation, introduces us to God's covenantal relationship with man in particular. In Genesis 2 the rest of the creation fades into the background while Moses focuses our attention on man as he is in relationship with God.

---

2. *The Westminster Confession of Faith* XXI par.vii.
3. For a discussion of these 'Creation Ordinances' see John Murray, *Principles of Conduct* (Grand Rapids: Eerdmans, 1964) 27-106.

Genesis 2 introduces us to the covenant that God made
with man in the garden and to the creation ordinances of
work, marriage and the Sabbath. These ordinances were
designed to regulate man's relation with God and his fellow
men. Let us look more carefully at the Sabbath ordinance.

God's rest

How did God establish Sabbath-keeping? He instituted the
Sabbath both by His example and by the words of institution.
First, He established the principle of Sabbath-keeping by
His resting on the seventh day: 'And by the seventh day
God completed His work which He had done; and He rested
on the seventh day from all His work which He had done'
(Gen. 2:2). The term 'Sabbath' is derived from the word
'rested' in verse 2.[4] By resting on the seventh day of creation,
God Himself established the principle and practice of
Sabbath observance. In order to understand the Sabbath
ordinance we need first to understand why God rested. There
are three reasons.

First, by resting God declared that His work as Creator
was completed: 'thus the heavens and the earth were completed, and all their hosts' (Gen. 2:1). The words 'heavens',
'earth', and 'hosts' encompass all the products of God's
creative work on days one to six. The 'heavens' refer to the
sky; 'the dry land' and 'the sea' to the earth; and 'hosts'
refers to all those things that God created as the inhabitants,
so to speak, of the heavens and the earth. And so the hosts
are the heavenly bodies – the sun, the moon, the stars and

---

4. Derek Kidner, *Genesis, An Introduction and Commentary* (Downers Grove:
Inter-Varsity Press, 1972) 53, '...literally "ceased"; from *sabat*, the root of
"sabbath".' Cf. Franz Delitzsch, *A New Commentary on Genesis*, 2 vols. (Min-
neapolis: Klock & Klock, 1978), I, 108,109.

the planets. But the hosts also include all the creatures (plants, fish, birds, animals, angels and man) which God placed in the creation. By resting on the seventh day, God declared His work of creation to be completed.[5]

God's rest, however, was not a cessation from all work. Jesus confirms this when He says in John 5:17: 'My Father is working until now, and I myself am working.' God continues to work in providence. *The Shorter Catechism* defines providence as 'His most holy, wise and powerful preserving and governing all His creatures and all their actions.'[6]

By His providence He governs the processes of life. The cycles of life continue with spring and autumn, sowing and reaping, birth and death. He providentially directs the formation of petroleum in the bowels of the earth, the birth of animals, the conception of babies in the wombs of their mothers, and the processes that lead to death.

Furthermore, God by His providence is directing the course of men and nations, bringing everything to the point of fulfilment when Christ shall come again to make all things perfect.

God also continues to work in redemption. From eternity He not only decreed the Fall of man, but also the salvation of His elect. Since the Fall, He has been working to accomplish that salvation.[7] He redeemed Israel, delivering them from the bondage of Egypt; He has established His church; and in the greatest deed of all He became a man and

---

5. The language does not mean that God completed His work on the seventh day, rather, by the conclusion of the sixth day He had finished His work of creation. See H.C. Leupold, *Exposition of Genesis*, 2 vols. (Grand Rapids: Baker Book House, 1970), 102; Delitzsch, 106,107

6. *Westminster Shorter Catechism* 11.

7. In Chapter 8 we will look the parallel between God's work of creation and His work of redemption.

lived on the earth in order to accomplish redemption. To this day He continues to work by calling His people unto Himself and sanctifying them. Thus God did not rest from all His work, but only the work of creation.

Since He continues to work, why this emphasis on rest? When God rested from the work of creation, He declared that it was completed exactly as He intended. Never again would there be need for this work. It is finished! He bids us to worship Him as Creator of heaven and earth.

Second, God rested *to express the delight He took in His creation*. Moses amplifies this concept in Exodus 31:17: 'It (the Sabbath) is a sign between Me and the sons of Israel forever. For in six days the LORD made heaven and earth, but on the seventh day He ceased from labor and was refreshed.'[8]

What a delightful phrase: 'God ceased from labor and was refreshed.' What does it mean? Did God need to rest because He was weary or tired? No! We know that He had not grown weary with His work of creation for He is omnipotent and unchangeable. He is the same yesterday, today, and forever. As Isaiah says in chapter 40:28: He 'does not become weary or tired'. Certainly God did not need to rest because His creative work wearied Him.

The refreshment of God on the seventh day was a refreshment of joy as He contemplated the beauty and the perfection of all that He had done. At the conclusion of the sixth day 'God saw all that He had made, and behold, it was very

---

8. The term 'refreshed' is an anthropomorphism, a figure in which God uses an analogy from our experience to give insight into his character or work. Since he does not need physical refreshment, we look for the analogy in our mental and emotional refreshment as we contemplate our work. See W. H. Gispen, *The Bible Student's Commentary, Exodus*, trans. by Ed vander Maas (Zondervan, Grand Rapids, 1982), pp. 290-291; James G Murphy, Commentary on the Book of Exodus (Klock and Klock, Minniapolis), pp. 341, 342.

good' (Gen. 1:31). On the seventh day God surveyed His work and took great pleasure in what He had made. His was a rest of joy, a rest of contemplation. Just as we step back to contemplate with joy something we have built or accomplished, God stepped back to contemplate His work with pleasure.

Third, by resting on the seventh day *God pictured the rest that He would provide for man*. He offered Adam and his descendants life (eternal rest). If Adam had not fallen into sin, he would have entered into that rest without passing through death. God, by resting on the seventh day, pictured the promised rest, so His rest was a type of our eternal rest.

This is why God does not record the end of the seventh day. The first six days were concluded by the cycle of evening and a morning, but the ending of the seventh day is not recorded. For Adam and Eve the seventh day concluded as had the previous day. The record of the day is left open-ended to picture the eternal rest that He would provide for His people.

By God's grace He did not cancel the offer of rest after the Fall. Rather, God renewed the promise of life, not through Adam's obedience, but through a Redeemer. According to God's eternal purpose the day of rest became a weekly promise and reminder to sinners that God would provide redemption and rest.

The fact that God's rest is a promise of eternal rest is confirmed in Hebrews 4:1-10 where the writer relates God's seventh day rest to the eternal rest that He has prepared for His people. Hebrews 4 teaches that God rested to symbolize the pattern of eternal rest that He was going to accomplish and establish for believers.[9]

---

9. See Chapter 8.

By resting, therefore, God declared His creative activity to be finished; He contemplated with joy the finished work; and He gave us a picture of the eternal rest that belongs to His people. By resting He gave us an example, reminding us that He is the all-powerful Creator who completed His work and thus has authority and power to govern it. He calls us to seek our rest in Him as we contemplate His goodness and grace in the beauty of creation and the wonderful offer of redemption. He promises the reality of entering into His eternal rest. In our Sabbath-resting we are reminded that God's works of creation and redemption are finished; we contemplate the complex beauty of His works and are refreshed in communion with Him; and we anticipate our eternal life with Him.

A day blessed and sanctified

Having taught these things by His own rest, God formally consecrated the seventh day for man to do these things. In addition to giving us the example of His rest, He *blessed* the day and *sanctified* it: 'then God blessed the seventh day and sanctified it, because in it He rested from all His work which God had created and made' (Gen. 2:3). In this dual action of blessing and sanctifying the day, God instituted the pattern of six days of work and a seventh day of rest.

Some suggest that God blesses the eternal rest and not the seventh day. In the Fourth Commandment, however, God bases our responsibility to sanctify the seventh day on His blessing of the Sabbath day: 'therefore the LORD blessed the Sabbath day and made it holy.' John Murray comments:

If this is true in the case of Exodus 20:11, the similarity of Genesis 2:3 would lead to the conclusion that in that verse also reference is made to the reason why the seventh day of our week is sanctified and blessed by God. In the transcendent realm of God's *opera ad extra*, on the grand plane of His creative action, He rested on the seventh day. God's mode of operation is the exemplar on the basis of which the sequence for man is patterned. There can be little doubt, therefore, that in Genesis 2:3 there is at least an allusion to the blessing of the seventh day in man's week; and, when we compare it more closely with Exodus 20:11, there is strong presumption in favor of the view that it refers specifically and directly to the Sabbath instituted for man.[10]

Furthermore, as we saw in the previous chapter, God's sanctification of the seventh day is the basis for His calling the day 'holy' in Isaiah 58:13. Therefore, God's acts of blessing and sanctification apply to the seventh day in our weekly cycle.

By blessing the day, God assigned to it a special purpose. In the creation account when God blessed something He both established purpose and endowed the thing created with the ability to fulfil that purpose. For example, when God blessed the animals in Genesis 1:22, He established their purpose of multiplying and filling the earth and endowed them with the desire and ability to procreate so that they might accomplish this purpose. Similarly in 1:28, He blessed man, giving him the purpose of multiplying, filling the earth and ruling over it. By means of this blessing He endowed man with the desire and ability to fulfil this task.

In like manner, when God blessed the seventh day, He gave it purpose and the ability to fulfil that purpose. He appointed the seventh day, the day He entered into His rest, to be a weekly pattern for the observance of His rest.

Furthermore, to those who would follow His example of

10. Murray, p. 32.

rest every seventh day He promised that He would bless
them. So by blessing the day He made the day a blessing for
man. Surely Christ had this in mind when He said, 'The
Sabbath was made for man and not man for the Sabbath'
(Mark 2:27).[11]

God's purpose in blessing the day is made clearer when
we understand what it means by His 'sanctifying' the day.
By this act He declared it to be holy. We have noticed that
when God sanctified something, He removed it from its
common use and set it apart for a special religious use
connected with His worship and service. We may assume
that in the same way that God set aside certain things for His
special use and service, He also set aside the seventh day
for the special purpose of worship and service. This is not
to deny that the other six days are holy and are to be used for
God's glory; for Christians are to glorify God in all of life –
everything they do is to be a holy service to the Lord. God,
though, establishes the seventh day as a special holy day for
special purposes.

By blessing and sanctifying the day God communicated
to Adam and Eve, and through the Scripture to us, the
principle of Sabbath-keeping. We are to treat as holy what
God declares to be holy. We may conclude that the observation of one day out of seven is a perpetually binding moral
obligation based on this creation ordinance.

The seventh day
Genesis 2:2-3 is a perpetually binding creation ordinance.
Some maintain that we are, therefore, obligated to observe
the *seventh* day. The problem arises from failing to observe
that certain moral laws have positive (temporary) elements

---

11. See Chapter 5.

attached to them that may be altered. Some of the Puritans referred to these as a moral-positive laws.[12] A moral-positive law is different from a simple positive law in that it joins certain elements to a moral law in order to give further instruction for carrying out the law. An example of positive law attached to a moral law is the law of consanguinity (regarding which relatives one may marry). The moral law for marriage as instituted in the creation ordinance and spelled out in the Seventh Commandment requires permanent, monogamous marriage. This law does not state that there is anything inherently sinful in one's marrying one's sister. So Cain and Seth were allowed to marry their sisters and Abraham his half-sister. Later, in the Mosaic law, God would forbid a man to marry his sister. Such a prohibition continues through the New Testament.[13] The moral law requires monogamous marriage; the moral-positive law regulates whom one may marry. The first law may not be changed, while the second was changed. The change with respect to whom one may marry does not detract from the permanent moral obligation of monogamous marriage.

With respect to the Sabbath, the moral requirement is for a regularly recurring amount of time to be allocated exclusively to God's worship. Specifying a day or a period of time is a moral-positive law. The changing of the latter does not affect the character of the former. Therefore, God may and indeed has changed the day.[14] *The Westminster*

---

12. James T. Dennison, Jr. *The Market day of the Soul* (New York: University Press of America, 1983) 78,79. Mr. Dennison draws these distinctions from Francis White, *Treatise of the Sabbath Day*, 28-33. See also John Owen, *An Exposition of Hebrews* (Marshallton, Delaware): The National Foundation for Christian Education, 7 Vol. 4, 1969) 327-332, 354-357.

13. *Westminster Confession of Faith* 24.4.

14. See Chapters 7 and 8.

Confession alludes to this when it refers to the Sabbath as 'a positive, moral, and perpetual commandment':

> The light of nature sheweth that there is a God, who hath lordship and sovereignty over all; is good, and doeth good unto all; and is therefore to be feared, loved, praised, called upon, trusted in, and served, with all the heart, and with all the soul, and with all the might... As it is of the law of nature, that, in general, a due proportion of time be set apart for the worship of God; so in His word, by a positive, moral, and perpetual commandment, binding all men in all ages, He hath particularly appointed one day in seven for a Sabbath...[15]

The Sabbath ordinance contained the positive law of one whole day in seven; that, from the creation, was the seventh day. But the day may be changed without affecting the inherent moral character of the ordinance.

We ought not to think of the Sabbath therefore as a temporary law, destined to pass away with the Mosaic covenant. Rather, as Dabney asserts:

> The reason that the ceremonial laws were temporary was that the necessity for them was temporary. They were abrogated because they were no longer needed. But the practical need for a Sabbath is the same in all ages. When it is made to appear that this day is the bulwark of practical religion in the world, that its proper observance everywhere goes hand in hand with piety and the true worship of God; that where there is no Sabbath there is no Christianity, it becomes an impossible supposition that God would make the institution temporary. The necessity for the Sabbath has not ceased, therefore it is not abrogated. In its nature, as well as its necessity, it is a permanent, moral command. All such laws are as incapable

---

15. *Westminster Confession of Faith* 21.1,7.

of change as the God in whose character they are founded. Unlike mere positive or ceremonial ordinances, the authority of which ceases as soon as God sees fit to repeal the command for them, moral precepts can never be repealed; because the purpose to repeal them would imply a change in the unchangeable, and a depravation in the perfect character of God.[16]

Others object at this point saying that God did not command Adam and Eve to keep the seventh day holy. Again we may refer to the parallel with the marriage ordinance in Genesis 2:22-25. When God gave Eve to Adam, He instituted marriage. Although God does not give a specific commandment about marriage, we understand that by this act He established marriage. Christ confirms this interpretation in Matthew 19:4-6:

> Have you not read, that He who created them from the beginning made them male and female, and said, 'For this cause a man shall leave his father and mother, and shall cleave to his wife; and the two shall become one flesh'? Consequently they are no longer two, but one flesh. What therefore God has joined together, let no man separate.

The institution of the Sabbath, like the institution of marriage, implies a commandment.

Still others object that there is no record of weekly Sabbath observance before Moses. John Murray effectively dealt with this objection when he wrote:

> Genesis is not silent. Genesis 2:2,3 proves that the Sabbath is a creation ordinance and, as such, must have been known to

---

16. Robert L. Dabney, *Lectures in Systematic Theology* (Grand Rapids: Zondervan, 1972) 379, 380.

Adam and his contemporaries. The silence of Genesis subsequent to Genesis 2:2,3 proves nothing as to the desuetude of the institution during patriarchal times, nor does it prove ignorance of the ordinance on the part of the patriarchs. But even if we suppose that the remembrance of this institution did pass away and that the patriarchs did not observe the weekly Sabbath, it is no more difficult to explain this lapse from the creation ordinance than it is to explain the lapse from the principle of monogamy so clearly implied in Genesis 2:24. It is precarious to base too much on silence. But even if the silence indicates declension, ignorance, and non-observance, this does not remove the creation ordinance nor does it disestablish its binding obligation.[17]

We, however, are not left to speculate. There are sufficient indications to suggest that the Sabbath continued to be an institution of patriarchal religion.

The least important evidence, mentioned by John Owen and R.L. Dabney, is the fact that seven has ever been a sacred and symbolical number among Patriarchs, Israelites and Pagans.[18] There is no natural phenomenon to suggest the symbolic significance of the number '7', but throughout the Bible the number '7' signifies perfection and sacredness.[19]

We also know that among ancient heathen there was the memory of the seventh day being sacred. Dabney quotes Clement of Alexandria as saying: 'That the seventh day is sacred, not the Hebrews only, but the Gentiles also acknowledge, according to which the whole universe of animals

---

17. Murray, 34, 35.
18. Robert L. Dabney, *Discussions: Evangelical and Theological* (London: The Banner of Truth Trust, 1967) 502, 503; John Owen, *Hebrews* I, 304-310.
19. J.D. Davis, *Davis Dictionary of the Bible* (Grand Rapids: Baker Book House, 1957) 546; J.D. Douglas, *The New Bible Dictionary* (Grand Rapids: Eerdmans, 1962) 898.

and vegetables revolves... Homer sings, "The seventh day then arrived, the sacred day." ' Again, 'The seventh was sacred... The seventh dawn was at hand and with this all the series is completed.' Clement also quotes the poet Callimachus as saying: 'It was now the Sabbath day, and with this all was accomplished. The seventh day is among the fortunate; yea the seventh day is the parent day.'[20] How then did this peculiar idea attach to the number, if not from the sanctification of the seventh day of the week at creation?

Further, Genesis 4:3 possibly refers to Sabbath worship when it says that at the end of days Cain and Abel brought their sacrifices. The 'end of days' is most likely the seventh day, the end of the week, the Sabbath day; so they presented their offerings to God on the seventh day.

In Exodus 16 we discover that Israel was aware of the responsibility of Sabbath-keeping before God gave them the Ten Commandments. When God gave the manna in the wilderness, He gave none on the Sabbath. Instead, He supernaturally preserved the manna collected on the sixth day. Manna was to be collected daily and it would not keep overnight. On the day before the Sabbath, however, they were to collect a double portion of manna and God promised to preserve the manna to be used on the Sabbath (verses 22-30). When questioned about this arrangement, God said: 'See, the LORD has given you the Sabbath; therefore He gives you bread for two days on the sixth day. Remain every man in his place; let no man go out of his place on the seventh day' (Ex. 16:29). This answer indicates that they were aware of the Sabbath.

That Sabbath observance was already known to God's people is further inferred from the language God uses in the Fourth Commandment. God calls on the people to 'Remember

20. Dabney, *Discussions*, 506.

the Sabbath'. Thus they were to call to mind what they already knew.[21]

Furthermore, as noted above, the Fourth Commandment is based on the creation ordinance: 'For in six days the LORD made the heavens and the earth, the sea and all that is in them, and rested on the seventh day; therefore the LORD blessed the Sabbath day and made it holy' (Ex. 20:11).

Thus we conclude that the concept of Sabbath observance is a moral law, based on God's creation ordinance. Keeping it is man's duty as a creature. As God delights in Himself, man is to pause to delight in God and worship Him.

Charles Hodge adds:

It appears, therefore, from the nature of this commandment as moral, and not positive or ceremonial, that it is original and universal in its obligation. No man assumes that the commands, 'Thou shall not kill', and 'Thou shalt not steal', were first announced by Moses, and ceased to be obligatory when the old economy passed away. A moral law is one that binds from its own nature. It expresses an obligation arising either out of our relations to God or out of our permanent relations to our fellowmen. It binds whether formally enacted or not. There are no doubt positive elements in the fourth commandment as it stands in the Bible. It is positive that a seventh, and not a sixth or eighth part of our time should be consecrated to the public service of God. It is positive that the seventh rather than any other day of the week should be thus set apart. But it is moral that there should be a day of rest and cessation from worldly avocation. It is of moral obligation that God and His great works should be statedly remembered. It is a moral duty that the people should assemble for religious instruction and for the united worship of God. All this was obligatory before

---

21. See Chapter 3.

the time of Moses, and would have been binding had he never existed. All that the fourth commandment did was to put this natural and universal obligation into a definite form.[22]

Having established that the Sabbath is a creation ordinance, we will look in the next chapter at the purpose of the Fourth Commandment.

22. Charles Hodge, *Systematic Theology*, 3 vols., (Grand Rapids: Eerdmans, 1975), III, 323, 324.

3

THE MARKET DAY OF THE SOUL
Exodus 20:9-11

We have looked at the Sabbath using the metaphor of a park in which we meet with God. Another picture for the Sabbath, one popular with the Puritans, was 'the market day of the soul'.

In Puritan England the market day was the chief business and social day of the week. Farmers, craftsmen, merchants, and housewives would come from the surrounding countryside and villages to buy and sell. Believing that God had appointed the Lord's day for especially important transactions with God, the Puritans called the Sabbath 'the market day of the soul'.[1]

Up to this point we have sought to demonstrate that Sabbath observance, far from being a legalistic bondage, is a glorious privilege with wondrous promises attached. Furthermore, in the last chapter we saw that God designed the Sabbath as a perpetually binding, moral obligation for all men and women everywhere.

Remembering the Sabbath
With these things in mind, we need to investigate the role of the Fourth Commandment in regulating the observance of the

---

1. James T. Dennison, Jr., *The Market day of The Soul: The Puritan Doctrine of the Sabbath in England 1532-1700* (New York: University Press of America, 1983) is an excellent study on the Puritan Sabbath.

THE MARKET DAY OF THE SOUL

Sabbath.[2] The Fourth Commandment, building on the creation
ordinance of the Sabbath, legislates how the day is to be struc-
tured, in the same way that the Seventh Commandment structures the creation ordinance of marriage and the Eighth
Commandment structures the creation ordinance of work.

By referring to the Sabbath as 'the market day of the
soul', the Puritans remind us that God gave us this day above
all other days to conduct spiritual commerce. The purpose
of the Fourth Commandment is to free us from our daily
business so that we may do business with Him on 'the market day of the soul'.

The Fourth Commandment states the purpose of the Sabbath by saying, 'Remember the Sabbath day to keep it Holy'.
The word 'remember' has a twofold significance. In the first
place God is saying, 'Don't forget or neglect it.' Often the
Old Testament writers used the word in this way. For example, in Exodus 13:3 Moses reminds the people not to
forget the historical act of their redemption, the Exodus:
'Remember this day in which you went out from Egypt,
from the house of slavery; for by a powerful hand the LORD
brought you out from this place. And nothing leavened shall
be eaten.' Christ uses a similar term, 'remembrance', this
way in the institution of the Lord's Supper, 'Do this in remembrance of me' (Luke 22:19).

The call to remember the Sabbath teaches that the Sabbath
as an institution had already been established. At creation
He made the day holy, and in the Fourth Commandment He
exhorts us not to forget that fact.

In the Bible, however, the term 'remember' means more
than not forgetting. It also means to observe and celebrate.

---

2. In the next chapter we will examine the unique role of the Sabbath in God's
covenant with Israel.

When asked 'Did you remember your anniversary?' the questioner is asking not only if you remembered the date, but if you did something special to celebrate the occasion? We 'remember' special occasions by giving gifts, going out to dinner or having a party. When God calls us to 'remember the Sabbath Day' He is commanding us to observe it in a special way; to commemorate it.

This concept of 'remember' is illustrated in Exodus 12:14: 'Now this day (referring to the day of the Passover) will be a memorial to you.' The noun 'memorial' comes from the same root as the verb 'to remember'. How was it a memorial? 'You shall celebrate it as a feast to the LORD; throughout your generations you are to celebrate it as a permanent ordinance.' Not only were they to remember the historical occasion, but also they were to celebrate by observing the Passover feast (cf. Exod. 13:3).

One 'remembers' the Sabbath by observing it according to God's regulation. It is for this reason, when Moses repeats the Ten Commandments forty years later, he uses the word 'observe' instead of 'remember'. 'Observe the Sabbath day to keep it holy ... therefore the LORD your God commanded you to observe the Sabbath Day' (Deut. 5:12-15).

When one rightly understands the significance of 'remember', one recognizes that the day was never merely a day of idle rest. Some suggest that the sole purpose of the Fourth Commandment was to provide physical rest for Israel. As God's rest, however, was not a rest of inactivity, neither is the rest commanded by the Fourth Commandment a rest of inactivity but of holy commemoration. According to Leviticus 23:2, 3, Sabbath rest entailed corporate worship:

Speak to the sons of Israel, and say to them, 'The LORD's appointed times which you shall proclaim as holy convocations – My appointed times are these: For six days work may be done but on the seventh day there is a Sabbath of complete rest, a holy convocation. You shall not do any work; it is a Sabbath to the LORD in all of your dwellings.'

A holy convocation was a time of corporate worship. Therefore, at least part of the purpose of the Sabbath rest was to observe the day by participating in public worship. So the term 'remember' teaches that the Sabbath is a day for holy transactions, a 'market day of the soul'. We remember the Sabbath day by keeping it holy.

A day special to God

God bases this exhortation on the special claim He has on the day: 'Six days shall you labor and do all your work, but the seventh day is the Sabbath of the LORD, your God.' God claims special proprietorship of the Sabbath. He owns the day and marks it as His by telling us how we may use it.

As noted in the previous chapter, this does not mean that we are not obligated to live all of life before God. Everything belongs to God and everything that we do must honour Him. Nevertheless, God marks this day as special and claims it for Himself.

Your house, like mine, belongs to God, and as Christians we are under obligation to use our houses for God's Glory. But our houses do not belong to God in the same way the church buildings belong to God. They were built by God's tithes and are to be used only for those purposes established by the Church officers. I cannot bring my bed and move in. They are holy in the sense that they are set aside for special uses related to worship.

Because the day belongs to God in a special sense, we are to remember it by keeping it holy. Properly used, the day enables us to remember God and His saving work. We are to treat the day as holy, sanctifying it as *The Shorter Catechism* teaches us:

> The Sabbath is to be sanctified by holy resting all that day, even from such worldly employment and recreation as are lawful on other days, and spending the whole time in the public and private exercises of God's worship, except so much as is to be taken up in the works of necessity and mercy.[3]

Keeping the day holy

What then are the transactions by which we keep the Sabbath day holy? First, we keep the day holy by actively resting in Christ ('holy resting'). The proper sanctification of the day, as with the proper observance of all God's commandments, begins in the heart, finding our rest in Jesus Christ. *The Heidelberg Catechism* says 'that all of the days of my life I rest from my evil works, let the Lord work in me through His Holy Spirit and so begin in this life the eternal Sabbath'.[4]

The Sabbath reminds us that we must cease from our own works, we cannot earn God's favour, we cannot work our way into heaven, nor can we merit righteousness. No, the Sabbath is our solemn confession and testimony that we rest in Jesus Christ alone for our salvation and we glory in Him. On this day we declare that He alone is our delight; He alone is our refuge and our hiding place.

Furthermore, we keep the Sabbath holy as we use it for

---

3. *The Shorter Catechism* 60. Chapters 10-12 will deal with ways to keep the day holy.

4. *The Heidelberg Catechism* 103.

communion with God. As we rest in Christ, we contemplate the beauty of God's attributes and the greatness of His work. We use the day, therefore, to have dealings with our Land-lord. We are His tenants who come on the market day to meet with Him. He holds court and gives us a return for our labour. He blesses us with refreshments and we feast at His table.

Sabbath observance is not to be a cold, ritualistic action we perform. Sometimes we think, 'Oh my, it is the Sabbath, I cannot do this' or, 'Oh, when will tomorrow come.' If you begin to grasp the privileges of the Sabbath as the market day of the soul, it will be your favourite day, better antici-pated than Saturday, more joyful than your birthday, more restful than a vacation. It is the Lord's day, and your first conscious thought ought to be, 'This is the day which the LORD has made; Let us rejoice and be glad in it' (Ps. 118:24).

Moreover, only as we approach the Sabbath in this man-ner will we avoid falling into legalism. Sometimes we ap-proach the Lord's day with a check-list of 'Do's and Don'ts', failing to realize that we can refrain from our work and rec-reation and perform all the correct things, but still be Sab-bath-breakers. It is only as we trust in Christ for the forgive-ness of our sins and the grace to obey that we can begin to keep the Sabbath holy. It is only as we approach the day out of love for God and communion with Him that we meet with God in the transactions of the day.

Further, we keep the day holy by devoting ourselves to the particular transactions that God has appointed. The most important of these is to meet with God in corporate worship. We supplement this with family and private devotions – read-ing, prayer and meditation. We take advantage of the day to spend it in fellowship with our Christian friends, as well as in works of ministry and mercy. By doing these things we make the best use of the day and get the most profit.

Dealing with the prohibitions

When we understand the great purpose of the Lord's day, we are in a better position to deal with the prohibitions of the commandment. As noted in Chapter 1, these prohibitions are not designed to rob us of pleasure, but rather to free us for the greater pleasure of the day. In our town there is a farmers' market every Tuesday afternoon. Two blocks of the city centre are closed to traffic so that the merchants may set up their booths in the street. Similarly, the Sabbath park is closed to regular traffic to allow for the market day of the soul.

The prohibitions of the Fourth Commandment teach us how to structure the day in order to derive the most benefit from it (verses 9, 10). God shows us how to structure our lives personally, domestically, and socially.

Personally, we are freed from our ordinary work: 'the seventh day is a Sabbath of the LORD your God; in it you shall not do any work.' The term 'work' includes all types of work. Verse 9 uses the word 'labour' which refers to manual labour – agricultural and other forms of labor that are performed by the hands. The term 'work', however, is more comprehensive, embracing not only the work described by 'labour' but also all business, trading and commerce, and domestic chores. By using both terms, God makes it clear that He prohibits all our regular work and activity.

Notice, though, that this prohibition is set against the backdrop of His giving us six days to do every kind of work: 'Six days you shall labor and do all your work.' We often focus on the deprivation of God's Commandments and fail to notice their wonderful blessings. God focuses on the two-fold privilege – six whole days to tend to all our labour and business and one whole day to devote ourselves to Him and His business. God gives us over 85 per cent of the week for our work and recreation. Although some take the phrase 'six days shalt thou labor' as a commandment that we must work at our vocation six days a week. I prefer to take this phrase as a concession. God grants you the use of six days for your work of all kinds. He also gives you one whole day to devote to enjoying Him. He is saying, 'I have given you six days; I require you to give Me one.'

Domestically, not only does God structure our occupational life for the market day, but He also commands us to structure our family life. Speaking to us in our roles as parents and guardians, He says: 'you or your son or your daughter.'

As parents we are to structure the lives of our covenant children so that they may be freed from work in order to devote themselves to the special transactions of the day. We are responsible for providing a positive and proper Sabbath-keeping structure for our children.

This means that we set an example of Sabbath-keeping for them. Moreover, we are to teach them what they should be doing, helping them to order their lives and schoolwork, and giving them only necessary chores around the house. We use the day as well to teach them that there is greater enjoyment in life than playing. Furthermore, we are to create for them a day they will enjoy, a day that they will anticipate, not a day that hangs over the week like an ominous, dark cloud.

Structuring of the Sabbath day also has a *social* responsibility. We are to structure the day for others in society for whom we are responsible. First, we have a responsibility to our servants. Not many of us have servants in our homes, but if we do, we are to release and protect them from unnecessary work in the same way we protect ourselves and our children.

Some of us, however, are employers, and economically our employees are our servants. As an employer you have the responsibility of not causing your employees to break the Sabbath by requiring them to do unnecessary work.

In another sense, all of us are indirectly responsible for some employees, specifically the people who are working in service industries and businesses. These people in economic terms work as servants for the consumer. I worked my way through college and seminary by selling shoes. My managers constantly stressed that I was a servant to the customer. Likewise those who serve us in the public sector are our servants. We are to protect their Sabbaths as well as our own. Thus we need to avoid shopping, unnecessary dining out,[5] and recreational activities that cause others to work on the Lord's day (this would include those events mediated by television, which necessitates hundreds of employees being at work). It is a lame excuse to say, 'They are going to be there anyway, so it really doesn't matter what I do.' You are commanded not to cause others to do unnecessary work. If you use a person's services, you are partly responsible for that person's working on the Lord's day.

Furthermore, as part of our social responsibility, God commands us to rest our animals because they need rest just as

5. I recognize that those who are on trips may have to eat in a public facility on the Lord's day, even as they may have to stay in a hotel. Interestingly the Puritans recognized this need as well. The Puritan-controlled Parliament in 1644, in a bill to regulate the Sabbath, added: 'Provided, and be it Declared, That nothing in this Ordinance shall extend to the prohibiting or dressing of Meat in Private Families, or the dressing and sale of Victuals in a moderate way in Inns or Victualling-Houses, for the use of such as otherwise cannot be provided for ....' quoted in Dennison, 94.

people do. Israel was an agrarian society and a good portion of their work was done with the aid of animals. God reminds us that He built into the fabric of creation the need for all living things to rest. Even the land was to rest (see Leviticus 25). The necessity of resting the land is illustrated by the importance of crop rotation that allows a portion of the land to lie fallow.

Surely, it is a fair inference to apply this principle to anything that can wear out. Just as employees have replaced domestic servants, machines have replaced animals. And like the living things they replace, machines wear out in proportion to use. Take for an example your automobile: the fewer miles, the better the resale value. If you were shopping for a used car and you found two cars of the same model and year, but one had thirty thousand miles and the other seventy thousand, which would you buy? In chapter 5 we will address the need for certain types of industry to operate seven days a week. A greater portion of industrial activities, however, could shut down on the Lord's day. What would be the economical and environmental benefits if they did?[6] Think of the extended life-span of expensive machinery, fewer repairs, and less pollution in the air and water.

Finally, as God teaches us how to structure His day socially, He includes those outside the church. He concludes by saying, 'your sojourner who stays with you.' In Israel the sojourner or stranger was the Gentile who lived in the midst of God's people. The reasons were many why Gentiles chose

---

6. Some, like Jewett, suggest that we ought not to promote the rest of the Sabbath on the basis of pragmatic or humanitarian benefits (*The Lord's Day*, p. 148). I would agree that such things ought not to be the basis of our argument, but God does call us to think of our animals. But, just as the laws concerning marriage, work and property have social benefits, it is important to recognize that the Sabbath also has social benefits.

to live in the land of promise. God commands that not only His people cease from labour, but also the non-covenant people in their midst. Interestingly, even though the stranger could not participate in the feasts or in temple worship, he had to cease from his work on the Sabbath.

Although we may not legislate that people go to church, may we not legislate that businesses and shops be closed on the Lord's day? Such laws, once prevalent in the United States and Britain, created an environment that was not only spiritually healthy but also mentally and physically beneficial.[7]

We have seen that the Sabbath is the 'market day of the soul'. God has appointed this day for special transactions with Him. As we structure the day accordingly, we will enjoy the benefits promised in Isaiah 58:13, 14. In order to free us for the pleasures of the day, God allows us to lay aside our normal, daily affairs so that we may devote ourselves to the sanctification of His day. In this we are reminded that, like all of God's law, the Fourth Commandment is not a burden but the way to true, balanced joy and happiness. We cheat ourselves and God when we use the day for our own work and recreation.

---

7. Some raise the question, 'What about those whose religion demands they observe a different day?' I recognize the tension here and do not have the final answer. But if we believe that God structures the day for the unconverted person as well as the Christian, we need to wrestle with this. Perhaps Jewish or Muslim-operated business could be allowed to operate on Sunday, but no Christian employee should be required to work, just as a Christian employer should respect the conscience of the person whose religious beliefs call for them to worship another day. The difficulty for adherents of other religions is not only with Sunday-closing laws. The laws of our land demand monogamous marriage, while Muslims and certain Mormons believe in polygamy. They are forced to conform to the laws of the land in which they live.

4

A SIGN OF THE COVENANT

We have considered the Sabbath as the 'market day of the soul' – a day appointed by God for special dealings with His people. It is for this reason we are to sanctify the day: that we might seek Him in it. Thus we are to structure the day first by ceasing from all unnecessary work. There are those, however, who suggest that as the market day, though useful for seventeenth-century England, has been made obsolete by malls, supermarkets and the internet, so the Old Testament Sabbath has been made obsolete by the work of Christ and the New Covenant. And, because the church worships on the first day and not the seventh, sabbatarianism is obsolete. We have a streamlined day for modern people. Others suggest that it is impossible for moderns to keep the Sabbath as required by the Westminster Standards. Thus, some contend, it is unbiblical and impractical to try to keep the Fourth Commandment. We will deal with the practicality of Sabbath-keeping in subsequent chapters. In this chapter, however, we will examine the question, 'Is the Fourth Commandment still binding?'

Anti-Sabbatarian arguments

Those who maintain that the Fourth Commandment no longer regulates our outward behaviour claim that the Sabbath was a covenantal sign for Israel alone and has now been done away with. They interpret the Fourth Commandment on the basis of Exodus 31:13-17:

But as for you, speak to the sons of Israel, saying, 'You shall surely observe My Sabbaths, for this is a sign between Me and you throughout your generations, that you may know that I am the LORD who sanctifies you. Therefore you are to observe the Sabbath, for it is holy to you. Everyone who profanes it shall surely be put to death; for whoever does any work on it, that person shall be cut off from among his people. For six days, work may be done, but on the seventh day there is a Sabbath of complete rest, holy to the LORD; whoever does any work on the Sabbath day shall surely be put to death. So the sons of Israel shall observe the Sabbath, to celebrate the Sabbath throughout their generations as a perpetual covenant. It is a sign between Me and the sons of Israel forever; for in six days the LORD made heaven and earth, but on the seventh day He ceased *from* labor and was refreshed.

The anti-sabbatarians assert that since the Sabbath was a sign of God's covenant with Israel, when that covenant was fulfilled in Christ and the New Covenant, the covenant sign of the Sabbath was abrogated. The weekly Sabbath, along with the Sabbaths of the religious festivals and the new moons, was a ceremonial ordinance which, like the sacrifices, was destined to pass away.[1] They will concede that there is a permanent moral principle requiring God's people to worship Him corporately, but insist that an entire day devoted to religious exercises is not required by the New Testament. Individuals may keep one day in a special way if they so desire, and the church needs an appointed day for worship, but the church may not command Sabbath-keeping nor should businesses be required by law to close. The state

---

1. For the exposition of this position see Gary D. Long, *The Christian Sabbath – Lord's Day Controversy*, Sovereign Grace Ministries (Stirling, VA: Grace Abounding Ministries, 1980); cf. D.A. Carson, *From Sabbath to Lord's Day.*

may not legislate morality or religious practice.

I do not disagree that the Sabbath system of the Old Testament had a special significance for Israel, but does the covenantal purpose of the Sabbath exhaust the purposes of the Fourth Commandment? Cannot the Fourth Commandment be a moral command and also have covenantal significance? We will look at a number of reasons why we must take the Fourth Commandment as a statement of moral law before examining its special role as a covenant sign for Israel. Finally we will consider how it continues as a sign and sanctifying influence for the New Testament people.

A statement of moral law

We begin by looking at the reasons for maintaining that the Fourth Commandment is part of God's moral law.

First, *the nature and unity of the decalogue (the Ten Commandments) teaches that the Fourth Commandment is an expression of God's universal moral will for all people*. The Decalogue serves as a summary of God's moral law. *The Larger Catechism* defines the 'moral law' as

> the declaration of the will of God to mankind, directing and binding everyone to personal, perfect, and perpetual conformity and obedience thereunto, in the frame and disposition of the whole man, soul and body, and in performance of all those duties of holiness and righteousness which he oweth to God and man: promising life upon the fulfilling, and threatening death upon the breach.[2]

In answer to the question 'Where is the moral law summarily comprehended?' the Catechism says:

---

2. *The Larger Catechism* 93.

the moral law is summarily comprehended in the Ten Commandments, which were delivered by the voice of God upon mount Sinai, and written by Him in two tables of stone; and are recorded in the twentieth chapter of Exodus. The four first commandments containing our duty to God, and the other six our duty to man.[3]

Advocates of the position that the Fourth Commandment serves only as a ceremonial sign for Israel claim that the Ten Commandments are not really a summary of moral law, but rather a statement of covenant law that God gave to Israel as his covenant people.[4]

The New Testament, however, is clear in its understanding of the Ten Commandments as a summary of God's moral law. For example, when Christ is asked what is the greatest commandment, He bases His answer on two Old Testament passages that summarized the Ten Commandments – Deuteronomy 6:5 and Leviticus 19:18:

You shall love the LORD your God with all your heart, and with all your soul, and with all your mind. This is the great and foremost commandment. The second is like it, You shall love your neighbor as yourself. On these two commandments depend the whole Law and the Prophets (Matt. 22:37-40).

In Matthew 19 Jesus shows the clear relationship of the second summary ('Love your neighbor as yourself') to the Ten Commandments. In answering the rich young ruler's question about which commandments he should keep, Jesus says:

---

3. *The Larger Catechism*, 98.
4. Long, p. 16-19.

> You shall not commit murder; You shall not commit adul-
> tery; You shall not steal; You shall not bear false witness;
> Honor your father and mother; and You shall love your
> neighbor as yourself (Matt. 19:18, 19; cf. James 2:8-11).

Here we see that Jesus considered the second greatest commandment to be a summary of the last six commandments.
Thus, if the summary is morally binding, that which it summarizes is morally binding as well.

Some respond that the last six commandments have moral
standing because they are repeated in the New Testament.
Jesus, however, in quoting the last six Commandments, recognizes the Ten Commandments as a summary of God's moral
law. Interestingly, while none of the first four commandments
is quoted in the New Testament, all four are alluded to and
applied there.[5]

As a summary of God's moral law, the Ten Commandments are a unified expression of God's will. This unity is
reinforced by the manner in which God gave the law (Deut.
10:4). The ten words which were given in such an awesome
manner at Mt. Sinai and which were engraved by the finger
of God in stone stand together as a unit. They could serve as
the basis of Israel's covenant relationship to God, because
they are the timeless expression of God's moral will. Therefore, it is contrary to all sound reason to dismiss one as
ceremonial and, therefore, no longer binding.

This is not to say that there are no ceremonial aspects to
the Fourth Commandment; all the ceremonial and judicial

---

5. Some claim that an Old Testament commandment must be repeated in the
New Testament in order to have a binding moral character on the Christian. They
say the other nine commandments are repeated in the New Testament while it
remains silent on the fourth. In subsequent chapters (5 and 8) we will show that
the New Testament is not silent about the Fourth Commandment.

laws of Israel are based on these ten commandments.[6] The 'ten words' summarized man's moral responsibility to God. The judicial laws applied the moral law to the civic life of Israel, while the ceremonial laws applied the moral law to her worship. All of the Ten Commandments have both civil and ceremonial ramifications. For example, the Second Commandment is applied to the entire system of tabernacle/temple worship, sacrifices, and religious festivals.[7] All of these things were types of Christ and His work, and would eventually pass away, but the moral requirement of the second commandment would remain.

As another example, consider the Fifth Commandment that promises prosperity and long life in the land God would give them (Deut. 5:16). In Ephesians 6:3 when the Apostle Paul repeats the promise he changes the wording to 'that it may be well with you, and that you may live long on the earth'. He alters the promise by taking away the theocratic element as it applied to Israel in the land, and adjusting the promise to New Testament covenant children.

Similarly there are ceremonial aspects to the Fourth Commandment – seventh-day worship, special Sabbaths, and feasts. These were exclusive to Israel and were destined to be fulfilled and thus abrogated in Christ. But the principle that God would have man devote one day in seven to worship and religious service is a universally binding moral law.

The second reason for considering the Fourth Commandment to be a moral law binding on all people and not just the

---

6. *The Westminster Confession of Faith* XIX.3, 4. I recognize that the distinction of moral, ceremonial, and judicial is not clear-cut in the Old Testament. This distinction, however, is valid as it notes the various ways the moral law was applied.

7. See Deuteronomy 12.

Israelites is *the scope of the commandment*: 'you shall not any work, you or your son or your daughter, your male or your female servant or your cattle or your sojourner who stays with you' (Ex. 20:10). As noted in the previous chapter, within the covenant context of Israel the stranger was the unconverted or, in some instances the converted but uncircumcised Gentile, who lived among God's people in the land. God obligated the unconverted Gentiles to observe the structure of the Sabbath, even though they could not take part in the feasts or in temple worship. We see the application of this prohibition in Nehemiah 13:15-21. Traders and merchants (at least some of whom were Gentiles, verse 16) were forbidden to conduct business on the Sabbath. Nehemiah threatened them with force if they persisted (verse 21). I chose this example since Israel, though still in covenant, was no longer an independent nation. She was a vassal state under foreign rulers. Nevertheless, Nehemiah applied the Fourth Commandment to Gentiles as well as Jews. From this we conclude that the Fourth Commandment was more than a sign of God's covenant with Israel. He required Gentiles living in the land to keep the law as well.

The third reason for recognising that the Fourth Commandment is a moral law and not a positive, ceremonial law is *the theological basis God gives for the commandment*. God declares that the ground for the Fourth Commandment is the creation ordinance: 'For in six days the LORD made the heavens and the earth, the sea and all that is in them and rested on the seventh day; therefore, the LORD blessed the Sabbath day and made it holy' (Ex. 20:11). This language clearly relates the Fourth Commandment to the pre-fall Sabbath ordinance.

Some suggest that as the deliverance of Israel from Egypt is given as the reason for the Fourth Commandment (Deut.

5:15), the creation ordinance cannot be the reason for the commandment. They say that if two different reasons were given, Scripture would contradict itself.[8]

The fact that the Bible gives two reasons for a law or an act of God in no way suggests confusion or contradiction. God often gives more than one reason for His acts. For example, Jude 7 states that God destroyed Sodom and Gomorrah for their gross immorality, while Ezekiel emphasizes their arrogance and oppression of the poor (Ezek. 16:49, 50). Is there any conflict in the two different stated reasons? No! Obviously God destroyed them for both types of wickedness. Jude wanted to emphasize one reason but Ezekiel the other.

There is no difficulty in God's giving two reasons for Israel to keep the Sabbath. In fact, as we noted above, the Ten Commandments, because they are a summary of God's moral law, can serve a special function for Israel as His covenant people. Therefore, God commands Israel to keep the Sabbath because Sabbath-keeping is part of the moral duty of all people. When they were about to enter the land He gave a second reason: namely, they were God's redeemed people.

Therefore, the evidence is clear that the Fourth Commandment, though containing a ceremonial element, is a perpetually binding moral obligation for all people. The market day is not outdated; it has moved from the city square to the new shopping centre, yet it still serves as the centre for our spiritual transactions with God.

But since the Fourth Commandment specifies the seventh day, are we not compelled either to keep the seventh day holy or to admit that the Fourth Commandment is dated and

8. Long, pp. 15, 16.

no longer binding? No, because we have already noted that the Fourth Commandment had ceremonial application. In Chapter 2 we saw that the particular day was a moral-positive law. Because it was a moral-positive law, the day can be changed without affecting the moral nature of the law.[9]

The Sabbath was a covenant sign for Israel

The Sabbath ordinance did play a special role for Israel as the covenant people. According to Exodus 31:16, 17 it served as a covenant sign:

> So the sons of Israel shall observe the Sabbath, to celebrate the Sabbath throughout their generations as a perpetual covenant. It is a sign between Me and the sons of Israel forever; for in six days the LORD made heaven and earth, but on the seventh day He ceased from labor, and was refreshed.

The moral obligation in its seventh day cycle, along with the other Sabbaths, would set apart the Old Covenant people.

As we noted in Chapter 2, before the Fall the Sabbath pledged the reality of eternal life. After the Fall it became a sign of the promise that God would provide eternal life for His people. For the Israelites the Sabbath sign pointed in two directions: backwards, reminding them of God as Creator who after the Fall had promised salvation through a Redeemer; and forwards, reminding them that they were to wait in faith for the promised Saviour.

Besides pointing back to creation and the promise of salvation, the Sabbath reminded Israel that God had delivered

9. Some argue that the Fourth Commandment only requires one day in seven and not the chronological seventh day. Exegetically I prefer the interpretation that refers to the seventh day as the seventh chronologically. Either way the moral nature of the commandment remains.

them from Egyptian bondage. In Deuteronomy 5, after repeating the Fourth Commandment as given at Mt. Sinai, Moses adds:

> And you shall remember that you were a slave in the land of Egypt, and the LORD your God brought you out of there by a mighty hand and by an outstretched arm; therefore, the LORD your God commanded you to observe the Sabbath day.

Once they had been enslaved; now they are about to enter into a rest in the promised land, which was itself a picture of their relationship with God. Not only were they not to oppress their slaves, but also they and their slaves were to observe the Sabbath. God marked the day of rest as a sign of the fact that they were the redeemed people of God for whom He was providing a rest.

By observing the Sabbath at the end of their week, Israel was taught to wait for God's deliverer, the true Rest-giver. Therefore Sabbath-keeping was a perpetual sign to them of what God had already done and would still do.

Moreover, it was a sign to the people who lived around them that Israel stood in a special relationship to God, having been set apart by and for Him. Time and again, when God calls His people to account for their apostasy, the one violation by which He summarizes their entire disobedience is Sabbath-breaking. By breaking the Fourth Commandment they desecrated and profaned the sign that separated them from the surrounding nations, designating them as the people of the LORD God, the redeemed ones (Ezek. 20:12, 20). As their males were marked by the sign of the covenant in their foreskin, the entire nation was marked by its Sabbaths.

The Sabbath was also a means of God's sanctifying work in the lives of His people. Through the Sabbath God declared: 'I am the LORD who sanctifies you' (Ex. 31:13). Sabbath observance contributed to their growth in holiness as it reminded them that they belonged to God – heart, mind and body. When they kept the Sabbath they knew they would enjoy the grace promised in Isaiah 58:13, 14.[10]

Furthermore, the seventh-year Sabbath and fiftieth-year jubilee not only typified the work of the Saviour to come (Luke 4:18), but also taught them to live by faith, trusting God for the promised harvest.

This unique role of the Sabbath in Israel's spiritual life, then, explains the strict enforcement of the sanction in Numbers 15:32-36. According to Exodus 35:1, 2, it was against the law to kindle a fire on the Sabbath because of the amount of work involved in starting a fire from scratch. We know that they were allowed to maintain fires since the priests kept the fire going on the altar (Lev. 1).

The man in Numbers 15 was gathering wood either to sell it or to kindle a fire. If the latter, he had not paid attention to his fuel supply and had neglected his fire so it went out. Furthermore, he had no need to collect wood to kindle a fire since he could have borrowed wood and some live coals from a neighbour or used a neighbour's fire. His wood-gathering was a public, flagrant disregard for God's law. In order to make unmistakably clear the importance of the law regarding the Sabbath, God had him put to death.

This episode does not teach, as some suggest, that we may not cook on the Lord's day or use electricity, although the application of the principle involved would preclude going out to buy groceries on Sunday, even if we had run out of food. Of course, the death penalty for Sabbath-breaking was a special part of the Mosaic economy which does not

10. See Chapter 1.

apply to us. The penalty, however, does teach the seriousness of the Sabbath. The church cannot remain faithful while
allowing a flagrant disregard for God's day.

A continuing sign

The fact that the Fourth Commandment was a sign for Israel
does not abrogate its moral obligation. The Sabbath continues to be a sign to God's covenant people in the New Testament. Just as the signs of circumcision and the Passover were
changed into the new covenantal signs of Baptism and the
Lord's Supper, the observance of the seventh-day Sabbath
has been changed to a first-day Sabbath and continues to
function as a sign for God's people.[11]

We who live in the full reality of accomplished redemption
have our Sabbath on the first day of the week to signify that
God has completed the objective work of redemption and
that we have begun to participate in that redemption. Like
Israel's Sabbath, ours also points backwards and forwards.
It points back to the resurrection of Christ and reminds us
that as we rest in Him, all our sins are forgiven. It also points
forwards, reminding us that Christ will return and we shall
live with Him in perfect bliss for evermore.

Our observance of the Lord's day serves also as a sign
and testimony to our neighbours that we belong to the
redeemed people of God. As we keep the Lord's day holy it
becomes a testimony to those around us that we are the special
people of God. Often there is little that distinguishes us from
our neighbours since many of them are outwardly moral,
responsible citizens and many attend church. One external
sign that God has given to us, the banner under which we
live, is the observance of the entire Christian Sabbath. By

11. See Chapters 7 and 8 for the change of day and its significance.

this we testify that we are not our own; we belong to the Lord. Our faithful Sabbath-keeping may be a testimony to our neighbours and our behaviour may give us opportunity to explain our practice to them. For example, when we tell a neighbour that our children cannot come to a birthday party or that we cannot take part in a neighbourhood outing or sports event because we are Christians and want to dedicate Sunday to God's worship and work, perhaps we will have an opportunity to explain more fully our reasons and faith.

It is paradoxical that those churches which talk the most about separation from the world most often teach against careful Sabbath observance. They express their separateness by conformity to a checklist of non-biblical laws: do not go to movies; do not drink; do not smoke, etc.

The Bible calls us to demonstrate our separateness by living according to the commands of Scripture, including keeping the Sabbath. We are not being legalistic when we observe the Sabbath carefully; rather we are demonstrating biblical separation. Legalism, by contrast, is adding to the law of God; trying to earn God's favour by our obedience; or trying to obey God's law apart from faith in Christ. We should note that conscientious precision in our obedience is not legalism.

A means of sanctification

Just as it did for the Israelites, the Sabbath also contributes to our sanctification. In Chapter 1 we dealt with the blessings attached to the Sabbath. To a great degree these blessings are related to our sanctification, a two-fold process of dying to sin and growing in holiness and obedience to God's Word.[12] Sabbath observance contributes to both of these

12. *The Shorter Catechism* 35.

things. In the first place it aids us in dying to sin. Because we have within us a remnant of sin, we must struggle daily against temptations and misordered priorities. We do not love the Lord our God with all of our hearts, minds, souls, and strength nor always seek first the kingdom of God and His righteousness. We forget the Lord in our work, in our hobbies, in our recreation, and in our use of possessions. We fail to trust in the Lord and begin to depend on others and the things of the flesh. The Lord has given us the Sabbath day to call us back to Him as our sovereign Master. This weekly punctuation of life that interrupts our work and pursuits of leisure and recreation, trains us to forget all else and look to Him. The Lord's day brings us into the presence of the Lord God, reminding us, 'Seek ye first the kingdom of God and His righteousness and all these things shall be added unto you.' The very practice of not pursuing our work and recreation and avoiding unnecessary thoughts and words about these things keeps us from becoming obsessed with them. It deals the death-blow to our becoming workaholics or to our being obsessed with our favourite recreation or activity. On this day God asks us to forget about everything else. Our propensity to idolatry is put to death. Thus the Sabbath sanctifies us in the negative sense.

Sabbath observance, however, also contributes positively to our sanctification. God promises in Isaiah 58, that if we keep the Lord's day holy, we are going to delight in the Lord and have spiritual prosperity and victory. The Sabbath is a means whereby we grow and prosper as Christians.

As noted in Chapter 3 the day is designed to contribute to our growth; for on this day the Lord gives us worship, teaching and preaching, and fellowship. He grants time to turn aside from other demands and preoccupations to read, study, and pray. He frees us so we can serve Him and our neighbour. All these things work in us to make us more like the Lord Jesus Christ.

Do we need these things any less than the Old Covenant people? The sign of the Sabbath remains, although the focus of its theological significance changes with the change of day. As circumcision is replaced by Baptism; the Passover by the Lord Supper; so the seventh-day Sabbath is replaced by the first-day Sabbath, the Lord's day.

Thus we have shown that the Sabbath, though serving ceremonial purposes, is a perpetually binding moral obligation. This interpretation is confirmed by the New Testament. In the next chapter we will begin our examination of the New Testament data about the Christian Sabbath.

5

THE LORD OF THE SABBATH
Matthew 12:1-8

My first church was in a small farming town in the state of Mississippi. Just north of the town the State Parks' Commission built a new kind of park called a 'living plantation'. The purpose of the park was to re-create a working nineteenth-century cotton plantation so people could experience what life was like on a southern plantation. In reality, however, the plantation is a museum and not a real plantation. Periodically, throughout the history of the church, leaders zealous for the Sabbath have turned the Lord's day into a museum; no longer the market day of the soul, it becomes a museum piece, a kind of 'living park'.

The Pharisees of Jesus' day had done this. When they came to prominence, the park looked like a desolate war zone. They led the restoration effort. They re-built the park, replanted all the flower beds, cleared all of the streams, and tended the grass and trees. They even put back the benches. Once again the park was a beautiful place. The people, however, were not allowed to benefit from the park. A fence was built around the park. They could come and see what the park was once like, in the way people today tour an old restored castle. It was like a museum.

But when the King's Son came to the city, one of the first things He did was to pull down the fence. He said, in effect, 'This park was designed to be used by My Father's people,

68

and I want to meet with them here.'

Jesus begins to pull down the fence in Matthew 12:1-8 (for parallels, see Mark 2:23-28; Luke 6:1-5). Many suggest that Jesus was doing away with the Sabbath, but in fact He comes as the Prince of Rest to re-establish the Sabbath as the day of spiritual rest for His people. Notice the relation of Matthew 11:25-28 and 12:1-8. The opening phrase of Matthew 12:1, 'at that time' or 'at that occasion' relates what follows to what precedes. Having given the great promise of rest (11:28), Matthew draws our attention to the day of rest.

We have examined the foundation of the Sabbath as it was laid in the Old Testament. We began by examining the great promise associated with the Sabbath in Isaiah 58:13 and 14. We learned that God intended from the beginning of man's existence for all people to keep one day in seven as holy; like marriage and work, the Sabbath is a creation ordinance. We discovered that in the Fourth Commandment God teaches us how to structure our lives in order to receive the blessings He has appointed. And we have sought to answer the objection that the Sabbath was a ceremonial sign for only the Old Covenant people and thus no longer binding on the people of God under the New Covenant.

In spite of what we have said thus far, many continue to object to the principle that the Lord's day is the Christian Sabbath. Objectors claim that not only does the New Testament never repeat the Fourth Commandment, but furthermore, Jesus himself repeals strict Sabbath-keeping.

In this chapter and the next three, we will examine these objections in light of the New Testament's teaching about the Sabbath. We begin with Matthew 12:1-8.

Jesus' teaching about the Sabbath

The first thing we see is Jesus Christ asserting His authority over the Sabbath. As Jesus and His disciples were walking through a grain field one Sabbath morning, His disciples became hungry and began to pick and eat some grain. Observing this, the Pharisees said to Him, 'Behold, your disciples do what is not lawful to do on a Sabbath.'

As their hatred for Jesus had intensified, the Pharisees had begun to follow Jesus in order to find fault with Him or His followers. Their vigilance was rewarded as they observed Jesus' disciples picking some heads of grain which they rubbed between their fingers to get rid of the husks, and popped into their mouths. Immediately, like bees to flowers, the Pharisees confronted Jesus. They were not accusing the disciples of stealing, for, according to Deuteronomy 23:25, it was permissible as one passed through a neighbour's field to pick some grain for a snack. Basically, they were accusing Jesus of allowing His followers to break the Sabbath, thus of promoting a disregard for the law.

Many mistakenly assume with the Pharisees that the disciples were violating the Sabbath. The disciples, however, were not breaking any Old Testament Sabbath laws. They were breaking only the man-made laws of the Jews.

The Pharisees' corruption of the law

The Pharisees and Scribes had a commendable zeal for the law of God. They loved the holy law and they wanted to protect it. Therefore they built fences around God's law to prevent people from transgressing it. In the same way that authorities put up barriers at dangerous places like the Grand Canyon to keep people from walking too close to the edge and falling over, the Jews devised laws to keep people far back from the dangerous precipice of violating God's law.

A contemporary example would be those churches that condemn all drinking because of the serious sin of drunkenness. They build a fence of man-made laws – no use of alcohol – to protect people from taking a step toward drunkenness. Eventually the humanly invented laws come to seem as binding as God's law, and ultimately, man-made laws become even more important than God's; in the words of Jesus: 'Neglecting the commandment of God, you hold to the tradition of men' (Mark 7:8). In effect, man-made laws to protect us from approaching sin deny the sufficiency of Scripture. Such laws strongly imply that God's Word alone is not able to teach us how to refrain from sin.

The Pharisees, the self-appointed guardians of God's law and particularly the Sabbath, devised hundreds of laws to keep people away from the cliff of violation. In the book of these laws, called the *Talmud*, they devoted twenty-four chapters to the Sabbath. They itemized some thirty-nine occupations, with multiple sub-divisions that might not be pursued on the Sabbath.

For example, the Fourth Commandment forbids any work at planting and harvest time (Ex. 34:21). On the basis of this prohibition the *Talmud* forbids picking grain (harvesting) and rubbing it between your fingers (threshing). So, the law the disciples broke was Jewish tradition, not God's law.

Jesus asserts His authority

Note that Jesus did not defend Sabbath-breaking, but the violation of tradition. In defending His disciples, Jesus Christ asserts His authority as the lawgiver and law-interpreter. When He says, 'For the Son of Man is Lord of the Sabbath,' He asserts His unique relationship to the law. He claims an absolute authority to interpret what is to be done on the Sabbath, and thus the right to tear down the fence. Jesus borrows the title 'Son of Man' from Daniel 7:13:

> I kept looking in the night visions,
> And behold, with the clouds of heaven
> One like a Son of Man was coming,
> And He came up to the Ancient of Days
> And was presented before Him.

Because of the Jewish misconceptions about the nature of the Messianic king, Jesus adopted this title to describe Himself as the Messiah. The title indicates His work of suffering as well as His exaltation as God's appointed Saviour-king.

His assertion, 'but I say to you' (verse 6) is reminiscent of His earlier claims in Matthew where Jesus repudiates the man-made interpretations of the Scribes and the Pharisees. He clearly states that He is not repudiating the Law of God:

> Do not think that I came to abolish the Law or the Prophets; I did not come to abolish, but to fulfill. For truly I say to you, until heaven and earth pass away, not the smallest letter or stroke shall pass away from the Law until all is accomplished. Whoever then annuls one of the least of these commandments, and so teaches others, shall be called least in the kingdom of heaven; but whoever keeps and teaches *them*, he shall be called great in the kingdom of heaven (Matt. 5:17-19).

Jesus asserts the beauty and integrity of God's law and its perpetual, morally-binding character. Consider that if Jesus Christ in His earthly ministry had contradicted the Law of God, He would have been discredited as the Messiah, for according to Psalm 40:6-8, the Messiah would come to do the will of God:

Sacrifice and meal offering Thou hast not desired;
My ears Thou hast opened;
Burnt offering and sin offering Thou hast not required.
Then I said, 'Behold, I come;
In the scroll of the book it is written of me:
I delight to do Thy will, O my God;
Thy Law is within my heart.'

Thus, in Matthew 5:17-19, after laying the foundation of the
eternal nature of the law of God, He does not repeal God's
law but rather the Pharisaical interpretations of God's law.
We see this illustrated in Matthew 5:21, 22:

You have heard that the ancients were told, 'You shall not
commit murder', and 'whosoever commits murder shall be
liable to the court'. But I say to you that everyone who is
angry with his brother shall be guilty before the court; and
whoever shall say to his brother, 'Raca,' shall be guilty before
the supreme court; and whoever shall say, 'You fool,' shall be
guilty *enough to go* into the fiery hell.

The Jews so narrowly expounded the Sixth Commandment
in terms of physical murder that they missed the heart of the
law. Jesus goes to the heart of the matter and teaches that
heart-actions like hatred or contempt violate the Sixth Commandment.

And so throughout Matthew 5, Jesus repudiates the false
interpretations of the Jews and asserts His true interpretation of the law. When He defends His disciples by asserting
that He is the Lord of the Sabbath, He is doing exactly the
same thing. He says, in effect: 'I alone am the authoritative
interpreter of the Holy Sabbath and its proper observance.'

Therefore, He is not abolishing the Sabbath, only the false

interpretations of the Sabbath. He re-establishes the day as
the time to celebrate the spiritual rest of His people. 'This is
the day which the LORD has made; let us rejoice and be glad
in it' (Ps. 118:24). Having proclaimed Himself as the promised rest-giver (Matt. 11:28), He begins to unencumber the
day of rest for its God-appointed purposes. Is this not appropriate as He restores the Sabbath as the day to celebrate
and commemorate our eternal inheritance? By our Sabbath-
keeping we declare that we have begun to participate in the
rest of eternal life, even as we press forward to enter into
that rest.

Before we leave this point of Jesus' authority, note how
often He deals with Sabbath observance. In the three years
of Christ's ministry recorded in the Gospels, on six different
occasions He crossed swords with the Jews over the proper
observance of the Sabbath. Furthermore, two of the occasions are recorded in three of the Gospels: the two accounts
in Matthew 12:1-14 are repeated in Mark 2:23-3:6 and Luke
6:1-11. Christ Himself taught six times about the Sabbath,
whereas He taught on only one occasion about murder and
three times on marriage. If this commandment were destined
for the dustbin of ceremonial law, why do the Gospel writers devote so much attention to it? Can you think of any ceremonial law regarding which Jesus spent so much time trying to correct people's practice? No, He prepared His people for doing away with the ceremonial law. But here He
clears away the rubbish; as the divine lawgiver, He pulls
down the fence and opens the park to be used properly by
His subjects.

The principles of piety and necessity

Having asserted His authority over Sabbath law, Jesus, the chief justice of the Supreme Court, examines the laws of the Jews on the basis of the intention of the King of the land and throws out as unconstitutional (unbiblical) every law that contradicts God's purposes for the Fourth Commandment. By His authority He establishes the principles by which the Sabbath should be observed, and teaches that we are to do those things that promote the purposes of the day. In His defence of the disciples, He spells out these principles, offering a series of biblical arguments to refute the traditions of the Jews.

Jesus draws His first argument from the history of God's covenant people (1 Sam. 21:1-6): 'Have you not read what David did when he became hungry? He and his companions, how they entered the house of God and they ate the consecrated bread which was not lawful for him to eat, nor for those with him, but for the priests alone?' The context tells us that David was fleeing for his life after Jonathan informed him that Saul intended to kill him. With a handful of followers, he left hastily without food or weapons. He sought food and a weapon from the priests at the tabernacle at Nob, but the only available food was the bread that had just been removed from the table of shewbread. Twelve loaves of bread were placed weekly on a table in the holy place of the tabernacle as a reminder that God was in fellowship with His people. On the Sabbath, the loaves were replaced with fresh bread, and the priests were to eat the week-old loaves (Lev. 24:5-9). Since this was the only bread in the house, the priest gave it to David and his followers.

Jesus chooses this account because of the parallels between David and his followers and Jesus and His disciples.

Since the shewbread was replaced on the Sabbath, we know
that both events occurred on the Sabbath. Further, both accounts deal with the Lord's anointed who is on the Lord's
business. Finally, neither instance was a matter of life and
death, but merely that the followers were hungry; they
strengthened themselves so that they might continue on the
Lord's business.

In this instance, Jesus argues from the lesser to the greater.
He implies that if it was proper to violate a ceremonial law
when the Lord's anointed was on the Lord's business on the
Sabbath, then surely the Anointed and His followers may
break a man-made law while they are doing the Lord's business on the Sabbath. From this first argument, Jesus teaches
that on the Sabbath we may do those things that strengthen us
for the Lord's work.

Jesus draws His second argument from the law itself.
Alluding to Numbers 28:9, 10, He says: 'Or have you not
read in the Law that on the Sabbath the priests in the temple
break (or profane) the Sabbath, and are innocent? But, I say
to you, that something greater than the temple is here.' The
priests not only had to work on the Sabbath, but in fact it
was their most intense work day. They offered double
sacrifices on the Sabbaths and continued all the other work
connected with running the temple: trimming the sacred lamps;
changing the bread of presence; performing all the other daily
rituals. Although a great deal of labour was expended in
tabernacle and temple Sabbath worship, the priests did not
violate the Sabbath law because their work was necessary
so God's people could worship.

Referring to the work of the priests, Jesus again argues
from the lesser to the greater because He is the fulfilment of
the temple as a type. He alludes to Himself in verse 6: 'But

I say to you, that something greater than the temple is here.'
That which the temple pictured and pointed to was the Lord
Jesus Christ, the temple of God who was tabernacling among
men. Therefore, those who laboured with Him in His Sabbath
work were not violating the Sabbath when they broke a
humanly invented law. To the contrary, they were doing the
true work of the Sabbath, as they laboured with Jesus in the
service of preaching, evangelizing and worshipping. They
were the true Sabbath keepers, while the Pharisees who
followed them seeking to entrap the Saviour were the ones
breaking the Sabbath.

Jesus draws His last argument from Hosea 6:6, when He
says: 'But if you had known what this means, "I desire compassion, and not a sacrifice," you would not have condemned
the innocent' (Matt. 12:7). He claims the innocence of His
followers by reminding the Jews that God is not looking for
heartless ritual on the Sabbath, but heartfelt worship; true
devotion that loves God and one's neighbour.

By establishing the innocence of His followers, He
condemns the Pharisees. Were they keeping the Sabbath
while they were sneaking around hoping to catch Jesus in
violation of their laws in order to discredit Him? Were they
busy about the things of God? Did they have hearts of
compassion for the people of God? Did they long to see the
worship of God advance? No, they were jealously guarding
their own little humanly invented rituals, while the innocent
were following the Lord of the Sabbath in service.

From this passage theologians have rightly derived the
principle that on the Lord's day we may do deeds of necessity. As *The Shorter Catechism* says: 'Spending the whole
time in the publick and private exercises of God's worship,
except so much as is to be taken up in the works of necessity

and mercy.'[1] John Murray specifies these works as deeds of piety, necessity, and mercy. To these we would add works necessary for preservation of life.[2]

Promoting the purposes of the day

In Matthew 12:1-8 Jesus teaches us that on the Lord's day, we may do those works of piety and necessity that promote the purposes of the day. We anticipated the purpose of the Lord's day as we looked at the purposes for God's resting in Genesis 2:1-3. In His rest, He did three things: He ceased from the work of creation; He refreshed Himself by the contemplation of that finished work of creation; and He pledged the rest of eternal life. Therefore, on the Sabbath, we are to cease from our regular labours and recreations so that we may contemplate with delight and be refreshed by the beauty of the Lord Jesus Christ our Saviour, in gratitude for His completed work and the rest He has provided for us. We devote ourselves to public and private worship, Christian fellowship, and service, in order to strengthen ourselves, advance His kingdom, and anticipate our heavenly rest with Him. Everything that we do needs to be examined in light of these purposes. How do our deeds promote the purposes of the day?

Many of us will be called on to do deeds of piety that are necessary to accomplish the purposes of the day. As the priests ministered in the temple, so ministers must preach and Sunday school teachers will teach. Someone will need to come early to turn on the heat or the air conditioner.

---

1. *The Shorter Catechism* 60.
2. This fourth category comes from the editor of a tract who published John Murray's address given at Golspie, Sutherland, August 12, 1953, reprinted *Collected Writings of John Murray* (Edinburgh: Banner of Truth, 1976), Vol. I: pp. 205-216.

Perhaps snow must be shovelled from the paths. All those things necessary to enable the congregation to gather for corporate worship, edification and fellowship are permissible.

Furthermore, when we understand the principle of necessity, we are able to apply it to the circumstances of our own lives. Everything we do should be measured by the question, 'Does this promote the purposes of the day?' Often we approach the Sabbath like children who push the rules of their parents as far as possible. We are like the boy who, when told he could not wear a particular shirt to school, put it in his gym bag and carried it to school, putting it on when he got there. Technically he did not disobey, since he did not wear it *to* school, but in reality, by wearing it at school, he disobeyed. Often this is how we approach the Lord's day. Rather than asking what may we do to please God and enjoy Him, we are asking, 'What can I do for my own pleasure? How far can I go without getting in trouble?' This attitude does not honour God. We should be asking if an activity will enable us to keep the Sabbath better, or if it will detract from the purposes of the day? We have a perverted legalism that is willing to live by the letter of the law but does no more in obedience than is absolutely necessary.

A proper grasp of the principle of necessity helps us to examine the various issues in our lives. For example, some say that *The Shorter Catechism* forbids physical rest when it requires 'spending the whole time in the publick and private exercises of God's worship ...'[3] Does this mean it is wrong to take a nap on a Sunday afternoon? To answer the question you must determine the purpose of the nap. Is it to refresh you so that you can pursue with renewed vigour the purposes of the day, or is it a choice of idleness because you

3. *Ibid.*, 60.

do not want to do anything else? Some people need a nap to stay awake for the evening service or to be able to read later without falling asleep. Others might need to go for a vigorous walk in order to be alert. Or, as mentioned earlier, our children often need some kind of physical activity so that the day will not be a burden for them.

This principle of necessity also helps us answer the question about the use of electricity. As noted in the previous chapter, our use of electricity is not forbidden by the prohibition to Israel about kindling a fire. A number of things necessary for a proper keeping of the Lord's day are provided by electricity. We need electricity to heat and cool our houses and church buildings and to provide light. Thus, it is not contrary to the principle of the Sabbath to turn on a light switch or a heater on Sunday.

Two cautions

We need to keep in mind, however, two cautions. First, we may not violate one of God's moral laws in order to keep another. We learn from the story about David and the shewbread that a positive law may be broken for higher purposes. But the Bible never suggests that we may break one moral law in order to keep another. For example, a group of pioneers, hiding from Indians, kill a crying baby because the noise of its cries exposes them to their enemies.

In applying this to the Sabbath, it is an improper rationalization to argue that we may go with our non-Christian neighbours to a ball game on Sunday in order to be able to witness to them. There is no warrant in Scripture for breaking the regulation of the Sabbath in order to pursue one of the purposes of the Sabbath – namely, seeking the lost.

Another example comes from a question I am frequently

asked as I teach on the Sabbath observance: 'I agree with everything you are saying, but sometimes I have to be in another city early Monday morning for business. Is it not better that I spend half a Sabbath with my family and fly on Sunday afternoon, rather than go on Saturday evening and be away from my family on Sunday?' When we understand that we may not violate God's regulation in order to fulfil one of the purposes of the Sabbath, our answer is clear. At all costs let us avoid being away from our families unnecessarily on the Lord's day, but if we cannot adjust our schedules, then we ought not to break the Sabbath in order to pursue the purposes of the Sabbath. In fact, if we use a portion of Sunday to travel, we are implicitly saying that the work of Monday morning is more important than the work of the Sabbath.

The second caution to keep in mind is that a work must be truly necessary for us to perform the God-ordained purposes of the Lord's day. For example, we noted that the Fourth Commandment prohibits our causing others to work on Sunday. If on Sunday morning I discover that I am out of milk, is it a necessity to go down to the grocery store and buy milk because I was negligent? No, it is not. My careless-ness put me into that situation. It is not carelessness that makes something a necessity, but its usefulness in enabling you to perform the purposes of Sabbath. On the other hand, if I am staying in a hotel over the weekend, it may well be a deed of necessity to eat in the hotel restaurant so I will have the strength to perform the duties of the day.[4]

Each of us will need to make his own decisions about what is necessary. Jesus gives us the criterion by which to

4. Some prefer to purchase sandwich material to keep in their room and others to spend the day in fasting. In my opinion, hotel/motel restaurants, like hospital or university cafeterias, are necessities in our society, but fast food establishments and restaurants not connected to a hotel/motel ought to be closed.

make these decisions: *Is this thing necessary to promote the purposes of the day?* We are to answer these questions for ourselves. If our desire is to fill the day with those things the Lord of the day has appointed, we will not be in danger of doing the unnecessary. In a sense, we should resent those things that divert our attention from profitable observation of the Lord's day.

Jesus Christ, the Lord of the Sabbath, tore down the fence of man-made law to free us to enjoy the purposes of the Sabbath. May God give each one of us the desire to seek and enjoy Him on this day. In the next chapter, we will look at those works of mercy and preservation that are permitted on the Lord's day.

6

THE SABBATH –
A DAY FOR COMPASSION

In our kitchen we have an antique chest called a 'pie-safe'. The chest, about six feet tall, has a mellow, natural wood finish. But the chest was not always as lovely as it is now. When we found it about twenty-five years ago it had a layer of white paint and over that a layer of pink paint and over that a layer of green paint. My wife and I spent hours stripping paint and sanding to get down to the bare wood. Afterwards we rubbed the wood with oil to bring back its natural lustre. We had to strip away about a quarter of an inch of accumulated dirt and paint to restore the chest to its original condition.

In the previous chapter we saw how the Pharisees, in order to protect the Sabbath day, had fenced it in. Although the purpose of the fence was to protect the day, it actually deprived God's people of the enjoyments and pleasures of the day. Christ, as the Son of the King, pulled down the fence so that people once again could come into the park.

The figure of dirt and paint removal is another way of thinking about what Christ did to restore the Sabbath for His people. The Sabbath is like a family heirloom, a beautiful piece of furniture that has been painted over by traditions. In Jesus' day it was so ugly that none could see its beauty or recognize the day as God had intended. Jesus scraped away all of the accumulated dirt and paint of human tradition and rules to restore the Sabbath to its original purposes.

Why did He do this? Why do the Gospel writers devote so much attention to the Sabbath controversies, if the Sabbath was to be done away with? Jesus spent little if any time correcting the Jewish ceremonial practices, while He spent more time teaching about the correct observance of the Sabbath than any other Old Testament commandment. He asserted His Lordship over the Sabbath in order to establish it as the appropriate day for the New Testament Church to celebrate and observe the rest that He provides. In Chapter 5 we learned from Jesus' defence of His disciples' picking and eating grain that we may do on the Sabbath those things that promote the purposes of the Sabbath; the deeds of necessity.

Confronting the Pharisees with regard to works of mercy
In this chapter, we will look at a second confrontation, recorded in Matthew 12:9-14. Although this confrontation occurred on a different Sabbath from the previous one, all three Gospel accounts group the two occurrences together in order to give us a comprehensive picture of Jesus' teaching concerning the Sabbath.[1]

In this account, Jesus teaches the principle that the Sabbath is a day for doing good to our neighbour. The event recorded in these verses is one of the classic spiritual confrontations between Jesus and the Jewish religious rulers. Knowing that He would come to the synagogue to worship, they set a trap. They knew where to find Jesus on the Sabbath. Since He kept the Sabbath faithfully, they knew they would find Him at the synagogue.

---

1. In the last chapter we noted the parallels in Mark 2:23-3:6 and Luke 6:1-11. Luke (6:6) tells us that it is another Sabbath.

Moreover, foundational to their plan was the assumption that Jesus was able to heal. What an amazing insight into the wickedness of their hearts and the depth of their depravity. They never stopped to ask, 'Who is this who can heal the sick, cast out demons, and raise the dead?'

The Pharisees elaborately set the scene. They positioned the man with the twisted, paralysed arm in a prominent place in the synagogue so that it would have been impossible for Jesus not to see the man or his tragic condition. As Jesus entered, they asked Him, 'Is it lawful to heal on the Sabbath?' In reality they cared nothing about Jesus' opinion, as they were looking for grounds to discredit Him. Furthermore, as we saw in the last chapter, at issue was not God's law, but their laws. According to their traditions, one could heal only if life were in danger. On another occasion, a ruler of the synagogue said, 'There are six days in which work should be done; therefore come during them and get healed, and not on the Sabbath day' (Luke 13:14).

The trap also depended on Jesus' character. They tacitly acknowledged not only His power, but also His compassion. They knew He would heal the man, for He never turned away the needy. Simply speaking, they had Jesus right where they wanted Him.

Jesus' response is amazing. Normally He avoided confrontation with His enemies. In fact, after the record of this controversy, Matthew applies to Him Isaiah's words found in Isaiah 42:1-3:

Behold my Servant whom I have chosen;
My Beloved in whom My soul is well-pleased;
I will put My Spirit upon Him,
And He shall proclaim justice to the Gentiles.
He will not quarrel, nor cry out;

Nor will anyone hear His voice in the streets.
A battered reed He will not break off,
And a smoldering wick He will not put out,
Until He leads justice to victory.
And in His name the Gentiles will hope (Matt. 12:18-21).

Jesus did not seek controversy with the Pharisees; when possible He avoided His enemies and did not claim openly to be the Messiah. Nevertheless, on this occasion He steps forward and provokes the Jews: 'He said to the man with the withered hand, "Rise and come forward!"' (Luke 6:8). Placing the poor man in the middle of the congregation, He asks, 'Is it lawful on the Sabbath to do good or to do harm, to save life or to kill?' (Mark 3:4).

Why? Why does the Saviour who is gentle and meek, who avoids confrontation, rise to their bait? He could have healed the man later, so why step into their trap? This question is all the more pertinent when we realize that in the majority of the Sabbath confrontations, Jesus took the initiative by deliberately healing on the Sabbath.[2] Why does He seek to provoke His enemies on this issue?

Obviously, the correct observance and use of the Sabbath is so important to Him that He aggressively seeks occasions to free the day from the laws of men by scraping away centuries of grime. On the basis of this observation it is incredible to think of the number of Bible teachers who claim that the New Testament is silent regarding the Fourth Commandment?

Jesus provokes the confrontation with a three-fold challenge, stated in a series of questions. Matthew does not record the first question, but uses it as a summary statement.

---

2. John 5:1-18; 9:1-14; Luke 13:10-17; 14:1-6.

According to Mark and Luke, Jesus first asks, 'Is it lawful on the Sabbath to do good or to do harm, to save a life or to destroy it?' (Mark 3:4) The Jews had asked Him, 'Is it lawful to heal on the Sabbath?' Jesus' question drives them back to the foundational, moral principle: 'Is it lawful on the Sabbath to do good or to do harm, to save a life or to destroy it?' Suddenly, they were caught in their own trap. The answer to His question was obvious; since it is never lawful to do harm or to destroy, they would have to say it is lawful to do good and to save a life. This answer is necessary because failure to do good is to do harm and the failure to save a life, when in one's power, is to destroy. This conclusion is based on a proper understanding of how to interpret biblical law; namely, the opposite of what is commanded is forbidden, and the opposite of what is forbidden is commanded.[3] For example, when God forbids adultery, He is requiring faithful, monogamous marriage.

Jesus rightly implies that if it is in one's power to do good, one must do it. Thus, if one has the opportunity within one's calling and circumstances to save a life but refuses, one is sinning. Since He could heal by the exercise of His will, when faced with proper circumstances it would be wrong for Him not to.[4]

His question silenced them, since to do that which is morally required cannot be a violation of God's Sabbath law. No wonder the Bible tells us they were silent and refused to answer Him.

---

3. *The Larger Catechism* 99, 'That as, where a duty is commanded, the contrary sin is forbidden; and, where a sin is forbidden, the contrary duty is commanded:...'

4. This statement applies to Jesus Christ who alone is sovereign in His ministry. The apostles and perhaps others during the Apostolic age could heal when Christ was willing. The gift of healing ceased with the Apostolic age.

He aims His second question at their wallets: 'What man
shall there be among you, who shall have one sheep, and if it
falls into a pit on the Sabbath, will he not take hold of it, and
lift it out?' (Matt. 12:11) According to their man-made laws,
although it was unlawful to heal on the Sabbath, if one's
livestock fell into a ditch, one could lower food and water
to it. Their laws made provision for getting an animal out of
a ditch on the Sabbath. He is asking, 'Do you do more good
to your livestock on the Sabbath, than to people?'

With His third question, in Matthew 12:12, Jesus springs
His trap, 'Of how much more value then is a man than a
sheep?' He says by implication, 'Your law allows you to
feed or save one dumb animal on the Sabbath, but forbids
one who has the divine power to heal a man.' On another
occasion, He phrases the question even more forcibly. After
healing the woman who had been bent double for eighteen
years, He answered the indignant synagogue official who
rebuked the people for seeking healing on the Sabbath:

> You hypocrites, does not each of you on the Sabbath untie his
> ox or his donkey from the stall, and lead him away to water
> *him*? And this woman, a daughter of Abraham as she is, whom
> Satan has bound for eighteen long years, should she not have
> been released from this bond on the Sabbath day? (Luke 13:15-
> 16).

The Saviour's spiritual logic is irrefutable – a person made
in the image of God, a member of the covenant people, is
infinitely more valuable than an animal. Again, by their
silence, the Pharisees admit the truth of His argument. Stating
the obvious conclusion in Matthew 12:12: 'So, then, it is
lawful to do good on the Sabbath,' Jesus healed the man.

The real Sabbath-breakers were the Pharisees. They were

angry not because He broke the Sabbath, but because He exposed their hypocrisy. Not only did they seek to hinder Him from doing good, but they were also seeking to destroy Him. Taking counsel with their arch enemies, the Herodians, they sought to do harm and destroy the One who did good and saved life, thereby breaking the Sixth as well as the Fourth Commandment. Technically, He did not break even their laws, since He performed no physical work, but healed by an exercise of divine power. They planned to murder Him because He exposed their hypocrisy.

Matthew concludes: 'So then, it is lawful to do good on the Sabbath.' In saying this, Jesus establishes the principle that the Sabbath is an appropriate day to do good. In fact this is part of the purpose of the day. What better day to do good than the day appointed by God to picture eternal life?

Jesus, therefore, does not do away with the Sabbath, but with the human accretions that made the Sabbath a burden. As He said earlier, 'The Sabbath was made for man, and not man for the Sabbath' (Mark 2:27). We learned in Chapter 2 that when God blessed the Sabbath, He made it a blessing for humanity. Thus, in addition to what we noted in the previous chapter (that deeds of piety and necessity are appropriate on the Sabbath), we learn that deeds of mercy and preservation are appropriate as well.

The principles of mercy and preservation

By way of application, first we rightly infer that those professions and deeds necessary for the protection of life and the promotion of the well-being of our neighbour are not inappropriate on the Sabbath. Those who work to do good, who protect and save life, such as physicians, soldiers, firemen, policemen, nurses and pharmacists, are not violating the Sabbath. A doctor ought not to schedule non-emergency surgery on Sunday, but in the case of a crisis, he will operate in order to save a life or protect someone from more serious danger or illness.

During war, a Christian general would prefer not to fight on Sunday, but may for strategic reasons conduct military operations on Sunday. By God's command, the army of Israel marched around Jericho seven days. Thomas 'Stonewall' Jackson, one of the great Christian generals of the Southern army in the War Between the States, was such a strict Sabbatarian that he would not read a letter delivered to him on Sunday. Thus, his wife was surprised when she read an account of a battle initiated by him on a Sunday. His answer illustrates a thoughtful application of the principle of necessity and mercy to military actions on the Lord's day:

> You appear much concerned at my attacking on Sunday. I was greatly concerned, too; but I felt it my duty to do it, in consideration of the ruinous effects that might result from postponing the battle until the morning. So far as I can see, my course was a wise one; the best that I could do under the circumstances, though very distasteful to my feelings; and I hope and pray to our Heavenly Father that I may never again be circumstanced as on that day. I believed that so far as our troops were concerned, necessity and mercy both called for the battle.... Had I fought the battle on Monday instead of Sunday, I fear our cause would have suffered; whereas, as things turned out, I consider our cause gained much from the engagement.[5]

Emergency repair work also may be considered as an act of mercy. Once when I had preached a sermon on the Christian

---

5. Mary Anna Jackson, *Memoirs of 'Stonewall' Jackson* (Dayton: Press of Morningside Bookshop, 1985) p. 249.

Sabbath, a young man who was a plumber expressed concern for what he should do when someone had a serious plumbing emergency on the Lord's day. If it is something that would cause no damage to the property, the work usually could wait until Monday, but if a pipe is broken or a sewage line is blocked, it is an act of compassion to repair the damage on the Lord's day, since the physical well-being of the people with the problem depends on it. Furthermore, they cannot enjoy the Sabbath with water ruining their home or sewage backed up in their bathroom.

And so the Sabbath is a day for doing those things that preserve life and promote the well-being of our neighbours. This exception does not apply only to human life. The Jews were correct to make provisions for their livestock. Farmers must feed their herds; dairymen must milk their cows; and the veterinarians will have to tend to sick livestock.

Note, however, an important caveat. Sometimes Christians appeal to this principle of 'the ox in the ditch' to rationalize inappropriate or unfinished work on the Lord's day. When I pastored in a farming community in Mississippi, farmers who professed to be Christians would sometimes work on Sunday. Their defence was to claim 'the ox was in the ditch'. This, however, is an abuse of the principle. The Bible clearly forbids the work of planting and harvesting on the Sabbath (Ex. 34:21). Christ's exception has to do with life in danger or our neighbour in need. The ox is not in the ditch merely because you are behind in your work. If nobody is about to die, no life is threatened, and no-one's neighbour is in serious need, the ox is not in the ditch.

A second application of the principle reminds us that the Sabbath is a day for doing spiritual good to our neighbour. Therefore, in addition to corporate worship and times of

private and family reading and fellowship, it is a day for
Christian service, for example, to do good by ministering in
nursing homes, visiting those who live alone or cannot get
out of their homes, and to do evangelism. Both the Early
Church fathers and the Puritans made provision for distrib-
uting food and money to the poor on the Lord's day, recog-
nizing that God designed this day for doing good.

A third application teaches us that we may do those things
necessary for the preservation of society at large. Some
postulate that since ours is a technical society and the Sabbath
was for an agrarian culture, it cannot be observed today.
Pointing to factories with large furnaces that cannot be shut
down on Sunday, they claim it is impossible to apply Sabbatarian principles to our technological society. In effect, those
who raise such objections are denying the sufficiency of
Scripture. Part of the work of theology is to discern the principles in the biblical account or narrative and to apply them
to modern circumstances.

Take, for example, the command to build a parapet around
one's roof (Deut. 22:8). A parapet was a wall or fence built
around a flat roof that served as a deck or balcony. Though
most of us do not have flat-roof houses, the principle still
applies that we are to take the necessary precautions so that
people are not injured on our property – for example, keeping a dangerous animal confined or fencing a swimming pool.

We, therefore, look for the principles of Scripture regarding the Sabbath that we must apply to our culture. One
principle is that when by nature an activity cannot be ceased
without affecting the work and livelihood of the other six
days, it may continue. I derive this principle from the life of
a crew on a ship at sea. Both Solomon and Jehoshaphat had
fleets of ships (2 Chron. 8:17, 18; 20:35, 36). A ship at sea

could not lie idle on the Sabbath. A number of necessary duties had to be done even on the Sabbath for the well-being of the crew: sails had to be trimmed, the course charted, general maintenance carried out and the physical needs of the crew met. In applying the principle we need to ask, 'Is the work necessary for the good or well-being of our neighbour and the continuance of his or our lawful calling?' Thus, the operation of a factory that cannot shut down without affecting its work for the remainder of the week is a deed of necessity, falling in the same category as an electrical generating plant, a hospital furnace room, or a college cafeteria. By employee rotation, no-one should have to work every Sunday and each ought to be able to attend morning or evening worship on the Lord's day.

A changed perspective

Jesus, the Lord of the Sabbath, scraped all of the ugly paint off this beautiful day. He pulled down the fence, not so you and I may do whatever we please, but to free us that we may enjoy the day and pursue its purposes – the worship of God, fellowship with Him and His people, and doing good to our neighbour.

On the basis of Jesus' teaching on the Sabbath, you can develop a philosophy that will guide your behaviour. Even if you are not convinced of the principles of strict Sabbath keeping, this philosophy will alter the way you regard what you do. It will re-orient you to seek to please God and to serve your neighbour. Your whole perspective will change.

I urge each one of you, whatever your view of the Sabbath, to examine your use of the day with these two sets of questions: First, does this thing you are doing promote the purposes of the day? Does it promote the cause of the gospel in your life and the lives of others? Does it promote the worship of God? If before God you can honestly answer 'yes' to that question, then do it to God's glory. If you cannot, then you ought to turn away from it. After all, is it not your desire to do those things that promote the cause of Christ and advance His kingdom, both in your life and in the world.

Second, is good being done to my neighbour – physically, and, more importantly, spiritually? What spiritual benefit is there for the waitress in the restaurant who has to work because churchgoers are eating there on Sunday? Does your act promote her salvation? Does your act free her to be able to worship? Is she able to enjoy the purposes of the day? The issue is not that she would be doing it whether or not you were there. The issue for you is whether you are doing those things that promote or hinder her spiritual well-being?' Apply that question to every decision you make, to every choice you contemplate, to everything that you do, because this is what we all should desire as Christians.

Having looked at the teaching of our Lord concerning the Sabbath, we will turn our attention in the next two chapters to the change of day.

7

THE DAY CHANGED;
THE OBLIGATION UNCHANGED
Colossians 2:16, 17

In the second century, a heretic by the name of Marcion taught a form of Christian gnosticism. He distinguished between the God of the Old Testament and the God revealed in Jesus Christ. He denied that Christ was a true man and he also rejected marriage. Since many of his doctrines were contrary to the Old Testament and portions of the New, he developed his own canon (the accepted books of the Bible). Marcion's Bible included only an edited Gospel of Luke and ten of Paul's Epistles. Needless to say, if one edits the Bible, one can get it to say whatever one wishes.

Today, countless numbers of Christians are editing their Bibles. Even though they theoretically accept the Old Testament as part of the Bible, they basically ignore its ethical teaching. They believe its history and point to its prophecies that have been fulfilled in Christ, but insist that its doctrines and commands must be repeated in the New Testament if they are to be authoritative for today's church. In effect, they excise from their Bibles a large portion of the Old Testament.

In response, Reformed, covenantal theologians affirm the unity of the Bible: whatever the New Testament does not repeal remains in effect. For example, much of what Christians believe and teach concerning marriage and family is revealed in the Old Testament. Our doctrine of the covenant and the place of our children in the covenant is based, in part, upon God's dealings with His people in the Old Testament Scriptures. Similarly, the foundation for the doctrine of the Sabbath as a Christian institution is laid in the Old Testament Scriptures. We have sought to establish from Genesis 2:1-3 and Exodus 20:8-11 that Sabbath observance is a permanent, moral requirement. This conviction is confirmed by the glorious promise of Isaiah 58:13,14. So, unless the New Testament repeals this ordinance, it remains in effect. Some suggest that Jesus did away with Sabbath observance in Matthew 12:1-14; we have seen, however, that Jesus restored the Sabbath and gave us helpful guidelines by which we are to examine our behaviour on that day.

The teaching of Paul

There are others who suggest that the apostle Paul repudiated the idea of Sabbath observance. These opponents of New Testament Sabbath base their arguments on three passages. The first is Romans 14:5, 6:

> One man regards one day above another. Another regards every day alike. Let each man be fully convinced in his own mind. He who observes the day, observes it for the Lord, and he who eats, does so for the Lord, for he gives thanks to God; and he who eats not, for the Lord he does not eat, and gives thanks to God.

The second is Galatians 4:10, 11:

> You observe days and months and seasons and years. I fear for you, that perhaps I have labored over you in vain.

The third is Colossians 2:16, 17:

> Therefore let no one act as your judge in regard to food or drink or in respect to a festival or a new moon or a Sabbath day, things which are a mere shadow of what is to come; but the substance belongs to Christ.

The opponents of Sabbath-keeping maintain that the New Testament church is no longer obligated to observe a special day, with some going so far as to say that to keep the Sabbath on the first day of the week is a form of Judaizing. According to them, Sabbath-keeping robs one of Christian liberty. An individual may observe a day as he wishes, but he may not require others to observe it.

This view is a misunderstanding of what Paul is saying in these passages. The key passage for understanding Paul's view is Colossians 2:16, 17. Not only does this passage help us understand Paul's approach to 'days', it also teaches that we may not observe the Jewish (or Judaic) seventh-day Sabbath. In other words, Paul abrogates the observance of the *seventh* day, but not the moral principle involved in the Sabbath command.

A quick glance at the context will aid us in rightly understanding Paul's prohibition. In the book of Colossians, Paul is counter-attacking a hybrid heresy that combined the Judaizer's doctrine of salvation by works which included observance of the ceremonial law, with the ascetic philosophy of gnosticism, which taught Christ was an emanation from God through a series of lesser divine beings, the worship of angels, and abstinence from certain foods and material and physical pleasures.

In Colossians 2, Paul establishes the supreme authority of the Lord Jesus Christ as Saviour and Lawgiver. He teaches that we do not serve Christ through obedience to man-made laws, traditions and ceremonies. Furthermore, we do not come to know God through the philosophy of the world, but rather through the revelation of God in the Scriptures. In light of these things he says, 'therefore let no one act as your judge in regard to food or drink, or in respect to a festival or a new moon, or a Sabbath day.' In the first half of the verse, he deals with the claim that because certain foods are unclean, the truly holy will abstain from eating them. Later Paul alludes to the ascetic doctrines he opposes:

> ... decrees such as 'Do not handle, do not taste, do not touch!' (which all *refer to* things destined to perish with the using) – in accordance with the commandments and teachings of men? These are matters which have, to be sure, the appearance of wisdom in self-made religion and self-abasement and severe treatment of the body, *but are* of no value against fleshly indulgence' (Col. 2:20-23).

In this passage, he repudiates all ascetic teaching about foods. The Scripture clearly teaches that a Christian may eat and drink in moderation anything God has given (Psalm 104:15; Mark 7:19; 1 Tim. 4:3-6).

In the second half of verse 16, Paul takes up the matter of days: 'therefore let no one act as your judge, in respect to a festival or a new moon or a Sabbath day.' Is Paul repealing Sabbath observance as such, or the observance of the seventh-day Sabbath along with the other ceremonial days? We find the answer to this question as we examine the three terms Paul uses: 'festival or a new moon or a Sabbath day (or Sabbath days).' These three terms are often used together in the Old Testament to describe the various ceremonial days that God's people were required to observe.

For example, 2 Chronicles 31:3, describing Hezekiah's reforms, says:

> He also *appointed* the king's portion of his goods for the burnt offerings, *namely*, for the morning and evening burnt offerings, and the burnt offerings for the Sabbaths and for the new moons and for the fixed festivals, as it is written in the law of the LORD.

And regarding Nehemiah's reforms, we are told:

> We also placed ourselves under obligation to contribute yearly one third of a shekel for the service of the house of our God: for the showbread, for the continual grain offering, for the continual burnt offering, the Sabbaths, the new moon, for the appointed times ... (Neh. 10:32, 33).

The Greek translation of these passages (called the Septuagint) uses the exact three terms that Paul uses in Colossians 2:16.

Leviticus 23 gives a detailed commentary on these terms. In this chapter, Moses sets out the entire liturgical calendar of the Old Testament church. Verses 1-3 deal with the weekly Sabbath:

> Speak to the sons of Israel and say to them, 'The LORD's appointed times which you shall proclaim as holy convocations – my appointed times are these: For six days work may be done; but on the seventh day there is a Sabbath of complete rest, a holy convocation. You shall not do any work; it is a Sabbath to the LORD in all your dwellings.'

In light of this, we see that Paul uses the term 'Sabbath days' to include the seventh-day Sabbath.

In verses 4 to 44, Moses explains the great festivals of

the Old Testament church: the Passover, coupled with the Feast of Unleavened Bread; the Feast of Pentecost; and the Feast of the Booths. Paul refers to these by the term 'feasts'.

Furthermore, in Leviticus 23:24, 25, Moses legislates special observances to be performed on the first of the month:

> Speak to the sons of Israel saying, 'In the seventh month on the first of the month, you shall have a rest, a reminder by blowing *of trumpets*, a holy convocation. You shall not do any laborious work, but you shall present an offering by fire to the LORD.'

Paul has this observance in mind when he uses the phrase 'new moons'. Thus by these three phrases, Paul is describing the Old Testament ceremonial days and Sabbaths and says that the Christian is under no obligation to observe these days.

This instruction was necessary in the time of transition from the Old Covenant to the New. Many Jewish Christians continued to observe the Old Covenant feasts and days. Although they were under no obligation to do so, since Christ fulfilled these observances, they worshipped Him through them. During this transition time, they were free to do so. Is this not what Paul was doing when he was arrested in Jerusalem (Acts 21:26)? Earlier, he had said he wanted to be back in Jerusalem in time for the Feast of Pentecost (Acts 20:16). Although Pentecost was not a Christian celebration, during the transition period from Old Covenant worship to New Covenant worship, the apostles and other Jewish Christians observed it to celebrate the saving work of Christ. In the same way, today some converted Jews often still observe the Passover in their families in order to reflect on Christ as the true Passover lamb.

A shadow of what is to come

Some, however, under the same misguided zeal that moti-
vated the Judaizers to require Gentiles to be circumcised,
were seeking to impose these days upon Gentile Christians.
In response, Paul repudiates any required observance of Jewish religious days or festivals, asserting that the Church may
not require the observance of any Old Testament ceremonial
day, because they were 'a mere shadow of what is to come;
but the substance belongs to Christ' (Col. 2:17). Paul reminds us that the Old Testament rituals foreshadowed the
person and work of the Lord Jesus Christ.[1] The person and
work of Christ stands behind all the Old Testament ceremonial observances: festivals, the new moon Sabbaths, and
the seventh-day Sabbath, as the divine original.

From eternity, God, having chosen us in Christ, planned
the incarnation and His great work of redemption. From the
beginning of history, when God began to reveal His truth,
God the Son in prospect of the incarnation towered over all
things. The light of revelation shone on Him and cast a
shadow across the events of Old Testament revelation. In
God's providence, the Old Testament worshipper could not
see Christ clearly; that sight was reserved for us who live in
the fullness of time (Heb. 1:1, 2; 11:39, 40). But through the
rituals and ceremonies they did see His mighty, majestic
shadow.

Thus, every part of ceremonial worship had reference to
the One who was the substance. The light of glory shone in
such a way on the pre-incarnate Christ that His shadow was
cast across the centuries through the sacrifices, tabernacle,
the temple, the priesthood, the schools of prophets, the kings

---

1. Joseph A. Pipa, Jr., *Root and Branch* (Philadelphia: Great Commission
Publications, 1989), chs. 7-10.

of Israel, the festivals, the new moons, and the Sabbath days.
Take, for example, the tabernacle and temple. John tells us
the Word became flesh and tabernacled among us (John 1:14).
Christ claimed to be the true temple (John 2:19), fulfilling
all that the temple promised. He is the true God dwelling in
the midst of His people. After His advent, the temple paled
into insignificance and was no longer necessary (John 4:21-
24), because with its festivals and sacrifices it was only a
shadow.

Similarly, each of the ceremonial days pointed to the Lord
Jesus Christ and His relation to His people. The Feast of the
Booths (also called Tabernacles) reminded them that God
was the God of salvation who had delivered His people,
and they were but pilgrims and sojourners in this land who
were moving on to a heavenly city, going from the shadow to
the reality. On the last day of the feast (called the eighth day
as a type of the resurrection), as the priest poured out water,
Jesus pointed to Himself: 'Now on the last day, the great day
of the feast, Jesus stood and cried out, saying:

> If any man is thirsty, let him come to Me and drink. He who
> believes in Me, as the Scripture said, 'From his innermost be-
> ing shall flow rivers of living water' (John 7:37, 38).

The Passover pictured Him as the Lamb of God who has
come to take away the sin of the world (John 1:29). Coupled
with this picture was that of the Feast of the Unleavened
Bread, a picture of His resurrection (1 Cor. 15:23). On the
very morning the priest stood in the temple and waved the
first loaves of barley bread, Christ came forth from the dead
as the first fruits of those who slept.

Pentecost, the great harvest festival, was the shadow of
the outpouring of the Holy Spirit and the gathering of the

nations unto the Lord Jesus Christ. At Pentecost the Jews observed the inauguration of the covenant at Mt. Sinai by which they were made the theocratic kingdom of God. Thus, Pentecost is fulfilled in the inauguration of the New Testament church with the outpouring of the Holy Spirit and the beginning of the world-wide gospel harvest.

Israel observed the new moon with special sacrifices and ritual. The first day of the month was regarded like the weekly Sabbath. The monthly recurrence of the moon probably reminded the people of the eternal certainty of God's covenant promises (Gen. 8:21, 22; Jer. 31:35, 36; 33:25, 26). Because Christ fulfilled all the covenant promises, He shall replace the light of the sun and moon (Rev. 21:23).

The most significant sign, however, was the seventh-day Sabbath. When Adam fell into sin, God gave the promise of the Saviour. Until He came, the Old Testament saints would remain under bondage, awaiting the day of their inheritance (Gal. 3:23-26). In their end-of-the-week Sabbath, they anticipated the coming of the Messiah who was to be the true rest-giver. Thus, the day of their Sabbath observance was a shadow of the Saviour's coming. When He came, He actually did part of His atoning work on the seventh-day Sabbath, by remaining in the tomb, suffering death and burial in the place of His people. When He rose on the first day, He entered in to His rest.

Although Paul does not mention the seventh-year Sabbath and the Jubilee, they too were fulfilled in Christ. As we noted in Chapter 4, the annual Sabbaths not only taught the people to trust God for their livelihood but also taught them to long for the day when the debt of sin will be remitted and the prisoners of sin set free. In Luke 4:18, 19, Jesus, quoting Isaiah 61:1, 2, applies the Jubilee language to Himself.

One day in seven – the continuing pattern

Therefore, the New Testament saint is no longer obligated to observe Old Testament ceremonial days and the Old Testament seventh-day Sabbath. But notice in this discussion that Paul never abrogates the moral obligation of keeping one day in seven. As we have seen, at creation God established the moral obligation of keeping holy one day in seven, and He reiterated this obligation in the Ten Commandments, along with all the other great moral principles of revealed religion. The particular day, however, was not part of the moral requirement of the law, but a positive law to regulate the fulfilling of the moral responsibility. Thus, the day of the week could be changed. The New Testament repeals the seventh-day observance, but never the obligation of keeping one day in seven as the Sabbath.[2]

Clearly, the early church continued to observe one day in seven. Why did they not adopt some other pattern like every third day or every tenth day? John Owen answers this question:

> And although absolutely another day might have been fixed on under the New Testament, and not one in a hebdomadal (seven day) revolution, because its peculiar works were not precisely finished in six days, yet that season being before fixed and determined *by the law of creation,* no innovation nor alteration would be allowed therein.[3]

Nor is there any evidence that some period of time elapsed between the practice of seventh-day worship and first-day worship. The New Testament church, keeping the pattern of one day in seven, immediately began to worship on the first

---

2. See H.C.G. Moule, *Colossians and Philemon Studies* (London: Pickering & Inglis Ltd) p. 175.

3. Owen, p. 362 (emphasis is mine).

day of the week. Furthermore, Paul's own practice confirms that he is not removing the observance of one day in seven but rather the Jewish ceremonial days. In Acts 20:7, he worships with the church of Troas on the first day of the week. In 1 Corinthians 16:1, 2 he intimates that he commanded all the churches to gather their offering for the poor on the first day of the week.

A proper understanding of Colossians 2:16, 17 also enables us to interpret Romans 14:4-6. In this chapter, Paul is discussing Jewish ceremonial laws. As in Colossae, some in Rome were advocating keeping certain Jewish food laws and holy days. Paul says that although people are free to observe Jewish food laws and holy days, they may not require others to observe such laws. Paul, therefore, removes any obligation to keep Jewish holy days.

Paul discusses the Christian's relation to Jewish ceremonial law in Galatians 4:10 as well. The list 'days, months, seasons, and years' refers to the various ceremonial observances of the Old Covenant people, part of that old system to which the Galatians were tempted to become enslaved.

Therefore, Paul never repeals the moral obligation of setting apart one day in seven to worship God. Rather, he abrogates the practice of Old Testament Sabbaths and ceremonial days. Let us summarize what we have said thus far with the words of R.L. Dabney:

The facts in which all are agreed, which explain the Apostle's meaning in these passages, are these: After the establishment of the new dispensation, the Christians converted from among the Jews had generally combined the practice of Judaism with the forms of Christianity. They observed the Lord's day, baptism and the Lord's supper; but they also continued to keep the seventh day, the passover, and circumcision. At first it was proposed by them to enforce this double system on all Gentile Christians; but this project was rebuked by the meeting of apostles and elders at Jerusalem, recorded in Acts 15. A large part, however, of the Jewish Christians ... continued to observe the forms of both dispensations; and restless spirits among the mixed churches of Jewish and Gentile converts planted by Paul, continued to attempt their enforcement on Gentiles also; some of them conjoining with this Ebionite theory the graver heresy of a justification by ritual observances. Thus, at this day, this spectacle was exhibited. In the mixed churches of Asia Minor and the West, some brethren went to the synagogue on Saturday, and to the church-meeting on Sunday, keeping both days religiously; while some kept only Sunday. Some felt bound to keep all the Jewish festivals and fasts, while others paid them no regard. And those who had not Christian light to apprehend these Jewish observances as non-essentials, found their consciences grievously burdened or offended by the diversity. It was to quiet this trouble that the Apostle wrote these passages. Thus far we agree.

We, however, further assert, that by the beggarly elements of 'days', 'months', 'times', 'years', 'holy days', 'new moons', 'Sabbath days', the apostle means Jewish festivals, and those alone. The Christians' festival, Sunday, is not here in question; *because about the observance of this there was no dispute nor diversity in the Christian churches*. Jewish and Gentile Christians alike consented universally in its sanctification. When Paul asserts that the regarding of a day, or the not regarding it, is a non-essential, like the eating or not eating of meats, the natural and fair interpretation is, that he means those days which were in debate, and no others. When he implies that some innocently 'regarded every day alike', we should understand, every one of those days which were subjects of diversity – not the Christians' Sunday, about which there was no dispute.[4]

---

4. Dabney, *Lectures*, pp. 385, 386 (emphasis mine).

Two lessons

Having established therefore the principle laid down by Paul, we may derive two very important lessons. First, Paul clearly asserts that the New Testament church may not observe the seventh-day Sabbath. Groups like Seventh-day Baptists and Seventh-day Adventists claim that since the Fourth Commandment is permanently binding, the church   must continue to observe the seventh-day Sabbath.

These groups maintain that the early church worshipped on the seventh day and only later under Constantine and the subsequent papacy was the day of worship changed to the first day of the week:

> ... people keep the first day of the week because the apostate church in the early ages borrowed this custom from the hea-then and handed it over to Protestantism. The heathen wor-shipped the sun on that day....
>
> Sunday has always been the day of heathen worship. It has always been dedicated to the sun god.... From the heathen practice of sun worship we get the word 'Sunday'. Speaking of the abominations being practised in the time of Ezekiel, the prophet said, 'And he brought me into the inner court of the LORD's house, and, behold, at the door of the temple of the LORD, between the porch and the altar, were about five and twenty men, ... and their faces toward the east, and they wor-shipped the sun toward the east' (Ezek. 8:16).[5]

Many Adventists interpret the seal on the 144,000 in Rev-elation 7 as seventh-day worship and view Daniel 7:25 as a prophecy of the apostate changing of the day from the sev-enth to the first.

Even if there were evidence that the early church (includ-

5. Richard Lewis, *The Protestant Dilemma* (Mountain View, Cal., 1961) pp.85, 141, quoted in Jewett, 113.

ing Gentiles) worshipped on the seventh day (and there is no evidence), one cannot escape the references to first day worship (Acts 20:7; 1 Cor. 16:1, 2; and Rev. 1:10). Nor can we escape the prohibition of Colossians 2:16, 17 to seventh-day Sabbath-keeping. For Adventists, unfortunately, the apostolic prohibition and practice carry no weight. One Adventist writer says: 'Let it be emphasized that even if apostolic support for Sunday were found, still the Bible Christian could not accept it. Not even an apostle could change the law of God.'[6] Such a cavalier approach to the New Testament is due in the main to their commitment to the prophecies of Ellen G. White. In their view these prophecies have divine authority and take precedence over apostolic practice. The clear teaching of the Bible, however, is that the seventh day has been abrogated.

The second lesson is very important for the whole discussion of on what day the Church is to worship. If Paul abrogates the seventh day but not the moral principle of one day in seven, how do we determine which day? We have two options: either the Bible reveals to us the proper day, or the church may choose the day. Many throughout the history of the church, including Calvin, have taught that since the church should have a day for worship, she may select the day. The Church appropriately chose the first day because of the resurrection. However, the implication is that the church is free to change the day if she so desires. Luther taught in his *Larger Catechism*:

But since the great majority are encumbered with business, there must be some day selected each week for attention to these matters. Since the harmless custom of the Lord's day

6. Lewis, p. 103 quoted in Jewett, 113.

has secured a unanimous consent, only confusion could result
from unnecessary innovation.[7]

Calvin expresses agreement:

Although the Sabbath has been abrogated, there is still occasion for us: (1) to assemble on stated days for the hearing of
the Word, the breaking of the mystical bread, and for public
prayers...; (2) to give surcease from labor to servants and work-
men.... Rather, we are using it as a remedy needed to keep
order in the church.... Also we should observe together the
lawful order set by the church for the hearing of the Word, the
administration of the sacraments, and for public prayers.[8]

As to the day, Calvin believed that the Apostolic Church
wisely chose the first day, because it was the day of Christ's
resurrection. But he says: 'Nor do I cling to the number
"seven" so as to bind the church in subjection to it. And I
shall not condemn churches that have other solemn days for
their meetings, provided there be no superstition.'[9]

But according to Paul in Romans 14 and Galatians 4, no
man or church has the prerogative to establish a day for others. Thus, if we are forbidden to worship on the seventh day
and may not legislate a day, the only alternative is that God
has legislated a new day. Quoting again from Dabney:

If we have been successful in proving that the Sabbath is a
perpetual institution; the evidence will appear perfect. The perpetual law of the decalogue has commanded all men, in all
time, to keep a Sabbath-day; and 'till heaven and earth pass,

---

7. Martin Luther, *The Large Catechism* (Philadelphia: Fortress Press, 1959), 20.

8. John Calvin, *Institutes of Christian Religion* (Philadelphia: The Westminster Press, 1967) II, viii, 32, 33, 34.

9. Calvin, II, VII, 34.

one jot or tittle shall not pass from the law of God till all be fulfilled.' The Apostle, in Colossians 2:16, 17, clearly tells us that the seventh day is no longer our Sabbath. What day, then, is it? Some day must have been substituted; and what one so likely to be the true substitute as the Lord's day? The law is not repealed; it cannot be. But Paul has shown that it is changed. To what day is the Sabbath changed, if not to the first: no other day in the week has a shadow of a claim. It must be this, or none; but it cannot be none; therefore it must be this.[10]

How then did God reveal to the Church the change of day? We will seek to answer this question in the next chapter.

---

10. Dabney, *Lectures,* 390, 391.

8

THE FIRST DAY SABBATH
Hebrews 4:9, 10

In the last three chapters, I have sought to remove the supposed New Testament objections to a Sabbath day. In Chapters 5 and 6 we looked at Christ's teaching and learned that He was not dismantling the observance of the Sabbath day, but rather the Jewish man-made laws that disfigured the day. In fact, Christ restored the day and gave us practical teaching on how to determine what is acceptable behaviour. In chapter 7 we examined Paul's teaching and discovered that he does not abrogate the moral principle of keeping holy one day in seven, but rather he abrogates the observance of the seventh day along with all other Jewish holy days.

Establishing the Christian Sabbath
If the obligation to observe one day in seven continues and we are not to keep the seventh-day Sabbath, what day ought we keep? Some suggest any day the Church prefers. Yet we affirmed in the last chapter that we may not determine the day, and that, in fact, from the apostles' time until now the nearly uniform practice of the Church has been Sunday worship. *The Westminster Confession of Faith* says that the day 'from the beginning of the world to the resurrection of Christ, was the last day of the week; and, from the resurrection of Christ, was changed into the first day of the week, which in Scripture is called the Lord's day, and is to be continued to

the end of the world, as the Christian Sabbath.'[1]

What was the basis of the change of day? We will attempt to answer this question by looking at Hebrews 4:9, 10.[2] These verses begin the concluding argument of the exhortation that begins in 3:7 and ends in 4:13.

The book of Hebrews was written to encourage Jewish Christians who were tempted to return to Judaism. It demonstrates that in Jesus of Nazareth God had accomplished His covenantal purposes. To prove this the writer demonstrates the completion of all of God's saving work in Christ. Richard Gaffin gives a helpful summary of this part of the message:

The opening words of Hebrews give a pronounced eschatological, redemptive-historical orientation to the entire document: God's former speech through the prophets, 'partial and piecemeal,' not only contrasts with but culminates in His final speech in His Son 'in these last days' (1:1-2). The present character of this 'last days,' eschatological revelation, embodied in the Son, is even more explicit in 9:26: In making sacrifice for sin, Christ has 'appeared once for all at the end of the ages'; in terms of the fundamental historical-eschatological distinction between the two ages. Christ's death and exaltation inaugurate the coming eschatological age. Accordingly, through God's word and the Holy Spirit the church already experiences ('tastes')

1. *The Westminster Confession of Faith* XXI, vii.
2. Andrew Lincoln teaches that the rest described in Hebrews 4 is the accomplished work of Jesus Christ. Believers have already come to the heavenly Jerusalem and although the rest will not be finalized until the second coming, there is nothing left for the believer to enter in to. Thus the Sabbath has been fulfilled and is abrogated: Carson, pp. 197-220. We will answer this objection indirectly in our development of Hebrews 4:9, 10. For a critical evaluation of Lincoln see the chapter by Richard Gaffin 'A Sabbath Rest Still Awaits the People of God' in *Pressing Toward the Mark*, ed. by Charles Dennison (Philadelphia: The Committee for the Historian of the Orthodox Presbyterian Church, 1986) pp. 33-51.

nothing less than 'the powers of the age to come' (6:5). Similarly, 'salvation' is a present reality resulting from God's eschatological speech 'through the Lord' (2:3; cf. 1:1-2; 6:9). Again, believers have already come to the city of the living God, the 'heavenly Jerusalem' (12:22) and are present in what is fairly described as the eschatological assembly gathered there (12:22-24).[3]

At the same time, however, the full reality is yet in the future, when Christ shall appear to make all things perfect (9:26). According to Gaffin:

> For believers that future, second appearance will be for 'salvation' (9:28, cf. 1:14; 6:9). A 'lasting city' is what they are still seeking; it is 'the city to come' (13:14; cf. the 'homeland' as well as the 'city' in 11:10, 13-16). The 'appearance' of the Son, salvation, the heavenly city (homeland), then, all eschatological in character, are both present and future in the view of the writer.[4]

This tension between the present and future nature of salvation gives rise to the theme of the book, an exhortation to the Jewish Christians to persevere. If they return to Judaism, they will be forsaking the full reality of the gospel for the shadows and types and will fail to enter into the rest of God. Of course, a true believer cannot fall away permanently, but the danger always remains that there are those within the church who, though professing faith, have not experienced the powerful salvation of God. A mere profession of faith does not save. True faith personally appropriates the promise of rest and manifests itself in perseverance.

The writer to the Hebrews points out the danger of failing to enter the rest by alluding to the apostasy of the children of

---

3. Gaffin, p. 34. 4. *Ibid.*

114 THE LORD'S DAY

Israel in the wilderness. Even though they had the promise
pictured by the seventh-day Sabbath and the offer of rest in
the land of Canaan, they failed to enter because of unbelief.
Furthermore, he reminds the Hebrew Christians that the rest
promised by God at creation in the establishment of the seventh-day rest was not fulfilled when Joshua brought them
into the promised land. He bases these conclusions on the
statement from Psalm 95:7-11:

> Today, if you would hear His voice,
> Do not harden your hearts, as at Meribah,
> As in the day of Massah in the wilderness;
> 'When your fathers tested Me,
> They tried Me, though they had seen My work.
> For forty years I loathed [that] generation,
> And said they are a people who err in their heart,
> And they do not know My ways.
> Therefore I swore in My anger,
> Truly they shall not enter into My rest.'

Since David wrote those words long after Joshua had led
the children of Israel into the promised land, he was showing that the rest in the promised land did not fulfil the promise of rest given at creation. Therefore, as long as the promise remained, there was an urgent necessity for God's people to appropriate that rest (4:7, 8). The fulfilment of God's
promised rest had been provided by Jesus Christ, and those
who believe in Him have begun to participate in its reality.
But they will participate in His rest only if they persevere
(3:6). If they turned back they would be like the children of
Israel who did not enter the land because of unbelief (3:16,
17; 4:1, 2). Like Israel in the wilderness, they were pilgrims.
They were to press on to the heavenly, eternal rest provided

by the Lord Jesus Christ: 'Let us therefore be diligent to enter into that rest' (4:11).

The author concludes his exhortation with 4:9-13. He introduces this section by saying in verse 9, 'There remains therefore a Sabbath rest for the people of God.' The word, 'therefore' introduces a conclusion to the argument of 4:3-8. The Hebrews were not to look back, but to look ahead, since there remains a Sabbath rest for the people of God. By referring to the people of God, the writer parallels the covenant people of the New Testament Church with God's people in the wilderness. He says the Sabbath rest with its promise of eternal life remains a reality for the New Covenant people of God.

Sabbath-keeping

The word translated 'Sabbath rest' (*sabbatismos*) is a unique word used only this one time in the Bible. The only other known possible use of the word is in Plutarch's *Moralia* in which, according to some versions, he uses *sabbatismos* to describe superstitious religious rest.[5] Thus the word suggests religious observances.

---

5. William F. Arndt and F. Wilbur Gingrich, *A Greek-English Lexicon of the New Testament and Other Early Christian Literature* (Chicago: The University of Chicago Press, 1957) p.746. Some critical editions of Plutarch suggest *baptismous* in place of *sabbatismous*. In this section, Plutarch is discussing barbarian superstitious practices, 'because of superstition, such as smearing with mud, wallowing in filth, Sabbath rests (*sabbatismous*) (or immersions, *baptisnous*) casting oneself down with face to the ground, disgraceful besieging of the gods, and uncouth prostrations.' Plutarch's *Moralia* section 166. Some scholars agree with the emendation, since 'resting' or even 'superstitious ease' (in Plutarch's view) cannot fit the context here with the mud packs and hurling to the ground to overcome fears and sleeplessness. In the previous sentence, however, Plutarch says they 'sit down on the ground and spend the whole day there.' The context at least suggests the possibility of the use of *sabbatismos*, spending a day in religious rest.

Although the noun form of the word used in Hebrews 4:9 is found nowhere else in the Bible, the verbal form of the word (*sabbatizo*) is used a number of times in the Septuagint.[6] The first use of the verbal form is in Exodus 16:30, 'So the people rested (sabbatized) on the seventh day'; that is, they observed a Sabbath rest. We learned in Chapter 2 that this verse concludes the section in which God tells them not to collect manna on the seventh day because it is the Sabbath (16:29). When they obeyed God and kept the Sabbath, they sabbatized.

This idea of Sabbath-keeping is involved every time this verb is used. For example, after a description of some feasts which were part of the worship of God's people, Leviticus 23:32 says, 'It is a Sabbath of complete rest to you, and you shall humble your souls; on the ninth of the month at evening, from evening until evening you shall keep your Sabbath.' The phrase 'keep your sabbath' is *sabbatizo*. In Leviticus 26:34, 35 the verb is used for the land's keeping its Sabbath rest (cf. 2 Chron. 36:21). In all the above instances the verbal form of *sabbatizo* is used to translate the Hebrew word meaning 'to keep the Sabbath'.

The early Christian writer Ignatius uses this verb to describe Old Testament Sabbath-keeping. In describing the change of day from the seventh to the first he wrote: 'no longer living for the Sabbath (*sabbatizo*), but for the Lord's day ....'[7] Therefore, the verb suggests a specific rest of Sabbath-keeping. Whether the noun *sabbatismos* was in existence or the writer to the Hebrews coined it, he would

---

6. Dr. S.M. Baugh, Associate Professor of Greek and New Testament at Westminster Seminary in California, suggests that the Septuagint translators coined this word to describe the activity of Sabbath keeping.

7. Ignatius, *Magnesians* IX,1.

have been familiar with the Septuagint's use of the verb *sabbatizo*. And, in either case, he chose this unique word with careful thought for a particular purpose.

Throughout Hebrews 3 and 4, the writer uses a more general word for 'rest' (*katapausis*)[8] to depict God's rest, the eternal rest to be entered and the typical forms of that rest as they are expressed in the seventh-day rest and the rest of Canaan. Why then does the writer select the unique word *sabbatismos* in verse 9?

He uses *sabbatismos* as a play on words. He emphasizes that the spiritual, eternal rest promised by God has not been fulfilled; the promise of eternal rest remains, and they must enter it by persevering faith. That is, one enters this spiritual rest by faith in the Lord Jesus Christ, but it will be fully realized only when one enters the eternal rest of glory. Thus, he emphasizes the ongoing need to persevere.

But if this were all he wanted to say, he could have used the word *katapausis*. In fact he uses *katapausis* this way in verse 11: 'Let us therefore be diligent to enter that rest (*katapausis*) ....' Nor does it make sense to say he chose *sabbatismos* for stylistic variety, as a synonym for *katapausis*. Such use does not make sense this late in the discourse. The uniqueness of the word suggests a deliberate, theological purpose. He selects or coins *sabbatismos* because, in addition to referring to spiritual rest, it suggests as well an observance of that rest by a 'Sabbath-keeping'. Because the promised rest lies ahead for the New Covenant people, they are to strive to enter the future rest. Yet as they do so, they anticipate it by continuing to keep the Sabbath.

Thus the theology of accomplished redemption does not

---

8. The noun *katapausis* (Heb. 3:11, 18; 4:1, 3, 5, 11); the verb *katapauo* (Heb. 4:8, 10). The Septuagint uses this word in Genesis 2:2 to describe God's rest.

annul a continued Sabbath-keeping, but requires it. And although we do not need a reinforcement or repetition of an Old Testament moral command, yet since the Sabbath did have ceremonial and typical significance, God gives clear New Covenant instruction. What better book to reiterate Sabbath observance than the book of Hebrews, which teaches most clearly how all Old Testament ceremonial worship practices were fulfilled in Christ and therefore repealed. A.W. Pink concludes:

Here then is a plain, positive, unequivocal declaration by the Spirit of God. 'There remaineth therefore a Sabbath-keeping.' Nothing could be simpler, nothing less ambiguous. The striking thing is that this statement occurs in the very epistle whose theme is the superiority of *Christianity* over Judaism; written to those addressed, as 'holy brethren, partakers of the heavenly calling.' Therefore, it cannot be gainsaid that Hebrews 4:9 refers directly to the *Christian Sabbath*. Hence we solemnly and emphatically declare that any man who says there is no Christian Sabbath takes direct issue with the *New Testament* Scriptures.[9]

---

9. A.W. Pink. *An Exposition of Hebrews*, 2 vols (Grand Rapids: Baker Book House, 1967) p. 210. Gaffin reaches the same conclusion, p.41: 'Certain effects, however, are unmistakable, or at least difficult to deny. [1] "My rest" (in its local character, see above) is a place of Sabbath-rest. In explicit fashion, reinforced by the use of Genesis 2:2 in verse 4 and verse 9 ties God's rest, in its sweeping, eschatological scope, to the institution of the Sabbath and its observance. [2] There is an inner connection between ongoing Sabbath observance and eschatological (Sabbath) rest; this ostensibly is the tie between anticipatory sign and reality. Although the writer does not say so explicitly, the clear implication is that recurring Sabbath observance has its significance as a sign or type of eschatological rest. [3] In view of the use of Genesis 2:2 in verse 4, it would appear to be the seventh *day* sign specifically, the typology of the *weekly* Sabbath, that the writer has in view, at least primarily.'

So, as the Old Covenant people of God had the promise of
future rest with its day of rest, the New Covenant people of
God, the church, also has the promise of future rest with its
day of religious rest.

Establishing the day

In addition to establishing the principle that there remains a
present Sabbath-keeping, this passage also establishes the
day of that Sabbath-observance. Verse 10 gives the grounds
and explanation for verse 9. Notice the writer says 'For',
which means 'because'. There remains a Sabbath-keeping
'because the one who has entered His rest has himself also
rested from his works as God did from His.'

In verse 10 the writer compares Christ's rest from His
work of redemption with God's rest from the work of
creation. Many commentators interpret verse 10 to refer to
the believer's turning from sin to rest in Christ.[10] The New
International Version translates verse 10: 'for anyone who
enters God's rest also rests from his own work, just as God
did from His.' The Revised Standard Version says: 'for
whoever enters God's rest also ceases from his labors as
God did from His.' The New American Standard Version is
closer to the original when it says: 'For the one who has
entered His rest has himself also rested from his works, as
God did from His.' The American Standard 1901 and the
Authorized Version (King James) are closest to the Greek:
'For he that is entered into his rest hath himself also rested
from his works (he also hath ceased from his own works
[King James]), as God did from His.'

---

10. For example John Calvin, *Calvin's New Testament Commentaries*, 12 vols.
(Grand Rapids: Eerdmans, 1970) 12:48, 49 and Andrew Lincoln in *From Sabbath
to Lord's Day*, pp. 213-214; 397.

John Owen offers three reasons for applying verse 10 to Christ's rest and not the believer's.[11] The first is the impropriety of comparing the believer's works and rest to God's work and rest. It is not proper to compare a sinner's works of sin and self-righteousness to the work of a holy God in creation. Gaffin points out:

> ... it (this interpretation) does not seem to perceive the jarring incongruity of drawing a direct (and therefore *positive*) parallel between man's sinful works and God's works. Where else does the New Testament even remotely approach the notion that 'repentance from dead works' is analogous to God's resting from His labors at creation? Does it really overstate to say that such a synthetic association is a glaring impossibility for any New Testament writer?'[12]

11. John Owen, *An Exposition of Hebrews* (Marshallton, Del.: The National Foundation for Christian Education, 1960, 7 volumes in 4) vol.2. Gaffin says 'To refer "the one who enters" to Christ [e.g., J. Owen ...], is not exegetically credible,' p.51 note 31. Gaffin, though, gives no reasons for rejecting Owen's arguments.

12. Gaffin, p. 45. Gaffin offers the interpretation that verse 10 refers to the positive works of a believer and that in heaven he shall rest from these (Rev. 14:13), 'In a word, the works of 4:10 are *desert*-works, the works of believers in the present wilderness, that is *non*-rest situation, looking toward the future, hoped-for, promised rest.' To do this he must interpret 'has entered his rest' as future. The problem with this interpretation is that it demands a future reference in the verb, but the verb for 'rested' is an aorist participle. Dr. Gaffin ascribes to this verb a 'generalizing or gnomic force' (p. 45). According to Burton the gnomic aorist 'is used in proverbs and comparisons where the English commonly uses a General Present'(Ernest de Witt Burton, *Syntax of the Moods and Tenses in New Testament Greek*. Edinburgh: T&T Clark, 1986. p.21). For New Testament examples see 1 Peter 1:24; Luke 7:35; John 15:6; James 1:11, 24. In a footnote Gaffin suggests also the possibility of a proleptical use. But as Burton points out, 'this is rather a rhetorical figure than a grammatical idiom' (p. 23). See, for example, 1 Cor. 7:28 'If you *should marry* ...' (NASV), cf. John 15:8 and James 2:10. Grammatically it is difficult to give any future force to this verb in its context. Dr. Baugh, in his unpublished class syllabus on Greek Verbal Aspect, writes of the substantive aorist participle (the form found in Hebrews 4:10): 'contrary to

As it is improper to compare the work of a sinner with that of God, it is also improper to compare the two rests. By referring to God's rest, the writer is building on Genesis 2:2,3; cf. Hebrews 4:4. God's rest was not only a cessation of specific activity, but also a joyful contemplation of His work. The believer's resting from his works is not a rest of contemplation and delight, but rather a sharp breaking-off with hatred from sin. Therefore, the parallel is not between the believer's resting from his works and God's resting from His.

Owen's second argument involves the change of pronoun. Throughout Hebrews 3:7-4:11, the writer refers to the rest of the believer in the plural: 4:1, 'Therefore, let *us* fear ...'; 4:3, 'For *we* who have believed enter that rest ...'; 4:11, 'Let *us* therefore be diligent ....' But in verse 10, he refers to an individual, 'The one who.' The use of the singular pronoun suggests someone other than the people of God, that is, an individual who has entered his rest as God has entered His.

Some suggest that the singular pronoun could refer to the antecedent 'people' in verse 9, since the Greek word for 'people' is collective (a singular noun referring to a group). Although 'people' may take a singular verb and a singular relative pronoun, the writer to the Hebrews defines 'peo-

---

expectations ..., aorist substantive and attributive participles most often (but not always!) refer to an event that is *past* in respect to the main action, whether the main action is past, present, or future from the writer's or speaker's perspective' (pp. 43, 44). In this case the phrase 'the one who has entered' precedes in time 'rested from his works', which is a past main verb. The other possibility is what Dr. Baugh refers to as 'inceptive'. 'With stative verbs (a verb like "rested" that expresses a condition or a state of being), the aorist substantive and attributive participles may express inception into the state' (p. 45). More than likely this is the force in Hebrews 4:10 'by resting he enters into a state of rest.' The action is still in the past. Furthermore, the development of the argument suggests a past tense for 'rest', since verse 11 exhorts the believer to enter into *that* rest. The phrase 'that rest' refers back to the rest established in verse 10.

ple' by the plural word 'brethren' (3:12). In Hebrews 7:5, in a similar grammatical construction, the writer defines 'people' by 'brethren' and uses the plural pronoun 'their' and a plural participle 'descended'. Furthermore, he uses the plural form of the pronoun used twice in verse 10, '*He* rested from *His* works' with the singular noun 'people' in 8:10. Thus, there seems to be no warrant relating the pronoun 'he' in verse 10 to 'people' in verse 9. Verse 10 is referring to an individual, whereas throughout 3:7-4:11 the responsibility to enter into the rest is addressed to the people of God in the plural.

This leads to the third argument. In verse 10, the writer describes a rest that is already completed, while in verse 11, he makes it quite clear that the responsibility to enter into the rest remains for the believer. Yes, we have begun to participate in God's rest, but we shall not fully enter into that rest until we are glorified with Christ in heaven. Gaffin recognizes this problem and seeks to interpret verse 10 as referring to a future rest. But this interpretation is grammatically unfeasible (see footnote 12).

Some object, 'Why an indefinite reference to Christ? Is it not awkward to introduce Christ in this fashion?' Christ and His rest are before us throughout this section. Remember the exhortation begins in 3:6: '... but Christ was faithful as a Son over His house whose house we are, if we hold fast ...' Verse 11 refers to 'that rest'; namely the rest provided by Christ. Furthermore, verse 14 reminds us that Christ has entered into His rest. Since grammatically one must take the entering as past and the impropriety of comparing the believer's resting from dead works with God's rest from creation, I see no other alternative than to interpret verse 10 in terms of Christ.

Creation and redemption

This understanding provides a parallel between the work of creation and the work of redemption. At the conclusion of creation, God rested on the seventh day to declare His work completed, to delight in that work, and to promise the eternal rest promised to Adam in the Covenant of Works. When Adam broke the covenant, God renewed the offer of eternal rest through a Redeemer. The seventh-day Sabbath looked forward to that rest.

God the Son rested from His work of redemption on the first day of the week as a sign that His work had objectively been accomplished and nothing remained to be done. In the resurrection He entered into the joy of His work and confirmed that eternal life had been purchased (Isa. 53:10, 11; Heb. 12:2). By His example, the day was changed. Vos wrote:

> Inasmuch as the Old Covenant was still looking forward to the performance of the Messianic work, naturally the days of labor to it come first, the day of rest falls at the end of the week. We, under the New Covenant, look back upon the accomplished work of Christ. We, therefore, first celebrate the rest in principle procured by Christ, although the Sabbath also still remains a sign looking forward to the final eschatological rest. The O.T. people of God had to typify in their life the future developments of redemption. Consequently the precedence of labor and the consequence of rest had to find expression in their calendar. The N.T. Church has no typical function to perform, for the types have been fulfilled. But it has a great historic event to commemorate, the performance of the work by Christ and the entrance of Him and of His people through Him upon the state of never-ending rest. We do not sufficiently realize the profound sense the early Church had of the epoch-making significance of the appearance, and especially of the resurrection of the Messiah. The latter was to them nothing less than the bringing

in of a new, the second, creation. And they felt that this ought to find expression in the placing of the Sabbath with reference to the other days of the week. Believers knew themselves in a measure partakers of the Sabbath-fulfilment. If the one creation required one sequence, then the other required another. It has been strikingly observed, that our Lord died on the eve of the Jewish Sabbath, at the end of one of these typical weeks of labor by which His work and its consummation were prefigured. And Christ entered upon His rest, so that the Jewish Sabbath comes to lie between, was as it were, disposed of, buried in His grave.[13]

The Old Testament alluded to the rest of the resurrection in the eighth day that climaxed the feast of the booths: 'For seven days you shall present an offering by fire to the LORD. On the eighth day, you shall have a holy convocation ... it is an assembly. You shall do no laborious work,' (Lev. 23:36). This high Sabbath at the end of the feast typified the rest promised to the pilgrim people. It was seen by many to conclude the annual cycle of feasts.[14] John apparently had this in mind when he referred to the first day of the week as the eighth day of the week in 20:26, 'And after eight days ...' As we shall see in the next chapter on the history of the Sabbath, the early church seized hold of the terminology of the eighth day to refer to the day of resurrection worship, the first day of the week. When the Church celebrated the resurrection of the Lord Jesus Christ, they related the joy of the eighth day to the declaration of Psalm 118:24, 'This is the day which

---

13. Geerhardus Vos, *Biblical Theology Old and New Testaments* (Grand Rapids: Eerdmans, 1968) 158.

14. Gustav Oehler, *Theology of the Old Testament* 2 vols. (Edinburgh: T & T Clark, 1883) II, 120. Cf. J.D. Davis. *Davis Dictionary of the Bible* (Grand Rapids: Baker Book House, 1957) p. 756.

the LORD has made; Let us rejoice and be glad in it.' Wilfred Stott gives the theological background:

> We must now, and in this connection, examine the origin of a very early name for Sunday, 'the Eighth Day'.... It seems more probable that we must look for the origin of the word in the Old Testament, inasmuch as the early church, having accepted the 'first day' as the occasion of the resurrection and of Christian worship, saw the connection of passages in the Old Testament in which 'first' and 'eight' are linked together. The most likely passage is ... Lev. 23:36-39. It is the description of the feast of Tabernacles. The first day and the eighth day are special days. On the first and eighth days there are to be 'holy convocations'. There is to be no 'laborious work' ... The days are a 'feast'... to the LORD, and there is to be 'rest'....The people are to 'rejoice' ... before the LORD ... There are other references to 'the eighth day' in other connections. It is of course connected with circumcision and entry into the Covenant ....
>
> It seems likely, therefore, that it was the influence of the Old Testament references to the eighth day and its accompanying festal character of joy and rest that affected early Christian thinking ... Is it too much to see in the second appearance of Christ to the gathered disciples in the Upper Room a hint of what set their minds in this direction?[15]

The first day of the week

As the apostles understood this theology by inspiration, they changed the day for celebrating the eternal rest from the seventh day to the first. The Old Covenant people looked forward to the accomplishment of redemption, so they kept the Sabbath at the end of the week. After the Rest-giver had accomplished His work, the New Testament Church kept its

---

15. Roger T. Beckwith and Wilfrid Stott, *The Christian Sunday: a Biblical and Historical Study* (Grand Rapids:Baker Book House, 1980), 64, 65.

Sabbath on the day He entered into His rest, signifying that although we wait for the consummation, we already have begun to participate in this rest.

The Church has always recognized that the change of day was first initiated by the resurrection appearances of Christ on the first day of the week when all of the New Testament's recorded appearances took place. Lange says with respect to John 20:26: 'That the disciples already attribute a particular importance to Sunday, is evidenced by the numeric completeness of their assembly.'[16] Philip Schaff, Lange's editor adds:

> This is the beginning of the history of the Lord's day, which to this day has never suffered a single interruption in Christian lands, except for a brief period of madness in France during the reign of terror. Sunday is here pointed out by our Lord Himself and honored by His special presence as *the day of religion, and public worship*, and so it will remain to the end of time. God's word and God's day are inseparable companions and the pillars of God's Church.[17]

This understanding is worked out in apostolic practice. In Acts 20:7 the Church gathered for preaching and the Lord's Supper on the first day of the week: 'And on the first day of the week, when we were gathered together.' Apparently it was their custom. Luke does not say 'on the first day of the week, when they gathered to say goodbye to Paul,' but 'on the first day of the week when we were gathered together to break bread, Paul began talking to them.' It was the custom of the early church to meet for worship on the first day of the week.

---

16. John Peter Lange. *Commentary on the Holy Scriptures* 12 vols. (Grand Rapids: Zondervan, 1976) IX, Part I, 621.

17. *Ibid.*, p. 621

In 1 Corinthians 16:1, 2, Paul assumes that the churches recognized the uniqueness of the day:

> Now concerning the collection for the saints as I directed the churches of Galatia, so do you also on the first day of every week; let each one of you put aside and save as he may prosper, that no collections be made when I come.

Just as it was the pattern in Galatian Churches, so also in Corinth they gathered for worship on the first day of the week, and took the collection for the poor. Paul does not instruct people to set aside money at home, because he wants to avoid having to make a collection when he arrives. He wants the church to make a collection on the first day of each week, which is another evidence that the Apostolic Church was committed to first day worship.

Thus the apostle John calls it the Lord's day: 'I was in the Spirit on the Lord's day, ...' (Rev. 1:10). The term John uses means a day that belongs peculiarly to the Lord Jesus Christ. It is not the often used phrase, 'the day of the Lord', but a term that means a day 'belonging to the Lord'.[18] This term is used only one other time in the New Testament, by Paul in 1 Corinthians 11:20 to describe the Lord's Supper. The Lord's Supper is not an ordinary meal, but a meal that belongs exclusively to the Lord, and was appointed to celebrate His redeeming work and to communicate grace to His people. In like manner, the first day of the week is called the Lord's day because it is a day that belongs peculiarly to the Lord and was appointed to commemorate His completed redemption and to communicate grace to His people.

18. William F. Arndt and F. Wilbur Gingrich, *A Greek-English Lexicon of the New Testament and Other Early Christian Literature* (Chicago: The University of Chicago Press, 1952) p. 459.

For these reasons also we worship on the first day and not on the seventh day. So also we learn from Hebrews 4:9, 10 that the practice of Sabbath-keeping remains for the people of God and they are to keep the Sabbath on the first day of the week. Dabney writes:

> The next place to be cited is Heb. iv. 9. This verse (with its context, which must be carefully read) teaches that, as there remains to believers under the Christian dispensation a hope of an eternal rest, so there remains to us an earthly Sabbath to foreshadow it. The points to be noticed in the explanation of the chapter are: That God has an eternal spiritual rest; that He invited Old Testament believers to share it; that it is something higher than Israel's home in Canaan, because after Joshua had fully installed Israel in that rest, God's rest is still held up as something future. The seventh day (verse 4) was the memorial of God's rest, and was thus connected with it. It was under the old dispensation, as under the new, a spiritual *faith* which introduced into God's rest, and it was unbelief which excluded from it. But as God's rest was something higher than a home in Canaan, and was still offered in the ninety-fifth Psalm long after Joshua settled Israel in that rest, it follows (verse 9) that there still remains a sabbatism, or Sabbath-keeping, for God's people under the new dispensation; and hence (verse 11) we ought to seek to enter into that spiritual rest of God, which is by faith. Now, let it be noted that the word for God's 'rest' throughout the passage is a different one from 'Sabbath'. But the apostle's inference is that because God still offers us His 'rest' under the new dispensation, *there remaineth to us a Sabbath-keeping under this dispensation.* What does this mean? Is the sabbatism identically our 'rest' in faith? But the seventh day was not identically that rest; it was the memorial and emblem of it. So now sabbatism is the memorial and emblem of the rest. Because the rest is ours, therefore the Sabbath-keep-

ing is still ours; heaven and its earthly type belong equally to both dispensations.[19]

Having sought to establish the moral obligation of New Testament Sabbath-keeping, let us now turn our attention to the use of the Sabbath for the New Testament people of God.

---

19. Robert L. Dabney, *Discussions*, 535.

9

A HISTORY OF THE PARK AND ITS USE

We all know that selected history can be twisted to prove almost anything. People often pervert history to fit their purposes in controversy. Nevertheless, history is a valuable record of God's providence and the chronicle of the beliefs and practices of the church. None should underestimate its importance or the lessons that may be gleaned from it. Needless to say, merely because influential, godly figures in the history of the church believed or did something does not make it correct, but history gives us the opportunity from which to look at Scripture by stepping outside our own culture to test our biases.

With these things in mind, I want to take you through a survey of the thought of the Christian Church on the Sabbath/Lord's day. We noted above that from the time of ancient Israel, people have wrangled over the use of the Sabbath. Today, those advocating the demise of the Sabbath often take their arguments from the history of the Church. How has the Church since the apostles viewed the day and its use? Were the Puritans who framed *The Westminster Confession* and *Catechisms* departing from the mainstream of the Church's teaching on the Lord's day? We will look briefly at the doctrine and practice of the Church up to the end of the Reformation. I will use the broad categories of the Early Church (100-500); the Mediaeval Church (500-1517); and the Reformation Church (1517-1700).

The Early Church

It is difficult to universalize the attitude of the early church on any issue. Those who lived closest to the apostles had the greatest difficulty in grasping the truth in a systematic fashion. They were, after all, pioneers – the first surveyors of the terrain, seeking to understand what Christ and the apostles taught. The task was enormous. The Bible is not a theological textbook, but a collection of history, poetry, prophecies and letters. The Church has the responsibility of searching the Scripture and systematizing its truth. Like a toddler, her earliest steps were often faltering. At times statements of the early Church fathers were at best ambiguous and at worse contradictory.

For example, early writers like Origen were unclear regarding the relationship of God the Son to God the Father. Not until the Council of Nicea in 325 did the Church clearly formulate an orthodox understanding of the deity of the Son, and decades passed before the issue was settled in the churches.

Clearly, this is the case with respect to the doctrine of the Sabbath. Some claim that the early church did not worship on the first day of the week until the time of Constantine in the fourth century. Others argue that, although the Church met on the first day of the week, it was only for the purpose of worship, and there was no commitment to spending the whole day in the worship and service of the Lord. I believe, however, that a careful reading of the early Church writers demonstrates not only first day worship but also a commitment to cease from work and to spend the whole day in worship and service. Admittedly a considerable number of early Christians were slaves who would not have been free in a pagan culture to do much more than worship. However, the community of believers' commitment was to keep the entire day holy.

Part of the disagreement arises because of the remarks of the early Christian writers against Sabbath-keeping. These statements were made in the context of a perverted Judaism. To the early Church Judaism was a Christ-denying, superstitious, legalistic religion. The early Christians mistakenly thought the Jews derived their practices from the Old Testament. In their polemic against the Jews, the Christians repudiated the Jewish Sabbath because they viewed it as part of the ceremonial system of the Old Covenant. Therefore, they often spoke despairingly of the Sabbath as part of their polemic against the Jews. The historian Philip Schaff, who edited the principle English edition of the *Church Fathers* says, 'There was a disposition to disparage the Jewish law in the zeal to prove independent originality of Christian institutions.'[1] Wilfred Stott writes of their attitude to the Sabbath, 'It was one of the signs of the Old Covenant with Israel .... The attitude of the Fathers is that with the passing of the whole system, temple, sacrifice, circumcision, clean and unclean, went the Sabbath as a sign ....'[2]

We see an example of this in Ignatius (*ca*. 100):

Be not led astray by strange doctrines or by old fables which are profitless. For if we are living until now according to Judaism, we confess that we have not received grace .... If then they who walked in ancient customs came to a new hope, no longer living for the Sabbath, but for the Lord's day, on which also our life sprang up through Him and His death ....[3]

---

1. Philip Schaff, *History of the Christian Church* in 8 vols (Grand Rapids: Eerdmans, 1985) vol.II, 202, 203.
2. Beckwith and Stott, p. 52.
3. Ignatius, *To the Magnesians,* ix.1.

Many early Church fathers viewed the Jewish Sabbath as part of the Mosaic bondage. Justin Martyr (*ca.* 100-165), in dialogue with a Jew, maintained that before Moses the patriarchs did not keep a Sabbath and that Christianity does not require one particular Sabbath, but a perpetual Sabbath, 'Moreover, all those righteous men, already mentioned, though they kept no Sabbaths were pleasing to God.'[4] He goes on to say that God gave them Sabbaths because of their hardness of heart.[5]

Irenaeus (115-*ca.* 200) wrote of Abraham, 'And that man was not justified by these things, but that they were given as a sign to the people, this fact shows, – that Abraham himself without circumcision and without observance of Sabbaths, "believed God, and it was imputed unto him for righteousness" ...'[6]

Tertullian (*ca.* 160-230) in *An Answer to the Jews* argues that the Sabbath was temporary and fulfilled with the coming of Christ:

> Therefore, since it is manifest that a Sabbath temporal was shown, and a Sabbath eternal foretold; a circumcision carnal foretold, and a circumcision spiritual pre-indicated; ... And, indeed, first we must inquire whether there be expected a giver of the new law, and an heir of the new testament, and a priest of the new sacrifices, and a purger of the new circumcision, and an observer of the eternal Sabbath, to suppress the old law, and institute the new testament, and offer the new sacrifices, and repress the ancient ceremonies, and suppress the old circumcision together with its own Sabbath ....[7]

---

4. Justin Martyr, *Dialogue with Trypho*, XIX.
5. *Ibid.*, XIX.
6. Irenaeus, *Against Heresies*, 4.16.2.
7. Tertullian, *An Answer to the Jews*, VI.

Furthermore, the Jews' misuse of the Sabbath was a recurring theme. 'The Jews are accused of spending the day in "inactivity".... Instead of using the day as it was intended by God in a study of the Scriptures and gaining knowledge, they spent it in idleness, dancing and in the pleasures of debauchery.'[8]

On the other hand, the early fathers believed that the Lord's day replaced the Sabbath. Schaff wrote:

> The fathers did not regard the Christian Sunday as a continuation of, but as a substitute for, the Jewish Sabbath, and based it not so much on the fourth commandment, and the primitive rest of God in creation, to which the commandment expressly refers, as upon the resurrection of Christ and apostolic tradition.[9]

Following the example of the Apostles, the early church replaced the seventh day worship with worship on the first day of the week. Schaff says that there is no doubt this change was of apostolic origin.[10] They referred to it as the 'First Day', the 'Lord's Day', and the 'Eighth day'. Justin Martyr said the Church met for worship on Sunday, the first day of the week:

> And on the day called Sunday, all who live in cities or in the country gather together to one place, and the memoirs of the apostles or the writings of the prophets are read, ... But Sunday is the day on which we all hold our common assembly, because it is the first day on which God, having wrought a change in the darkness and matter, made the world; and Jesus Christ our Saviour on the same day rose from the dead.[11]

---

8. Beckwith and Stott, p.51, 52.
9. Schaff, II, p. 202.
10. *Ibid.*, p. 201.
11. Justin Martyr, *Apology* I, 67.

Understanding that the day belonged in a special way to the Lord, the Church immediately adopted the phrase of the apostle John, 'Lord's Day' (Rev. 1:10).[12] In *The Didache* (early second century) the term 'Lord's Day' is used to describe the day of worship: 'On the Lord's day of the Lord, come together, break bread and hold Eucharist, ...'[13] Ignatius relates the Lord's day to the completed work of Christ: 'If then they who walked in ancient customs came to a new hope, no longer living for the Sabbath, but for the Lord's day, on which also our life sprang up through Him and His death ....'[14]

The third term used to highlight the importance of the first day is 'eighth day'. The *Epistle of Barnabas* refers to the Sunday by this designation. Speaking to express the attitude of the Lord, the writer says: 'The present Sabbaths are not acceptable to me, but that which I have made, in which I will give rest to all things and make the beginning of an eighth day, that is the beginning of another world.' The writer continues: 'Wherefore we also celebrate with gladness the eighth day in which Jesus also rose from the dead ....'[15] As noted in the last chapter, the early church derived this title from John 20:26. Lee observes on this section of *Barnabas*:

Apart from the rest of this Epistle, ch. 15 is striking evidence that 'the eighth day' (i.e. Sunday – cf. John 20:1, 19 & 26) was already being 'kept' ('agomen'), that the day already had strong soteriological and eschatological significance, and that it was even then regarded as a memorial of the Lord's resurrec-

---

12. See Chapter 8.

13. *The Didache* 14. For discussion of the textual variants see Nigel Lee, *The Covenantal Sabbath* (London: The Lord's day Observance Society, 1966) 298, 299.

14. Ignatius. *Magnesians* 9.

15. *Barnabas* XV.8,9.

tion (cf. John 20:1), and possibly of His post-resurrectional Sunday appearances too.[16]

In connection with the concept of the eighth day, the early church emphasized the festive character of the Sabbath; a holy festival, celebrating the resurrection of the Lord Jesus Christ.[17]

Although the term 'Sabbath' would not be regularly used for the 'Lord's Day' until after Constantine, there are a couple of references to the Lord's day as the Sabbath. Eusebius (*ca.* 260-339), in a commentary on Psalm 92, shows the relation of the seventh-day Sabbath to the Lord's day, 'The Word has exchanged and transferred the feast of the Sabbath to the Lord's day.'[18] Stott says:

> It is clear that there are mystical elements in it, but the references to "intervals of six days", "gatherings around the world", the allusions to the Eucharist, including the bread and "the blood of the Lamb which taketh away the sin of the world", the emphasis on "each Lord's day several times", all suggest that it is a literal Sunday which Eusebius has in mind.[19]

Earlier, Origen (*ca.* 185-254) refers to the Lord's day as the Sabbath. In the *Homilies on Numbers*, quoting Hebrews 4:9, he says, 'Leaving the Jewish observance of the Sabbath, let us see how the Sabbath ought to be observed by a Christian.'[20] He then continues to discuss how the Sabbath should be spent. Stott says, 'While elsewhere Origen clearly saw the Sabbath as a type of the rest from sin and evil works of

---

16. Lee, p. 241.

17. Beckwith and Stott, p. 64.

18. Eusebius, *Commentary on the Psalms*, quoted in Beckwith and Stott, p.75ff.

19. Beckwith and Stott, p. 77.

20. *Ibid.*, p. 70.

all kinds, here he is dealing in a practical way with the observance of the Christian festal day.'[21]

For Origen the Christian Sabbath was to be kept by abstaining from work and recreation:

> Leaving the Jewish observance of the Sabbath, let us see how the Sabbath ought to be observed by a Christian.... On the Sabbath day all worldly pleasures ought to be abstained from. If therefore you cease from all secular works ... and execute nothing worldly, but give yourself up to spiritual exercises, repairing to the church ..., attending to sacred reading and instruction, thinking of celestial things, solicitous for the future, placing the judgment to come before your eyes, not looking to things present and visible, but to those which are future and invisible, this is the observance of the Christian Sabbath.[22]

The highlight of the day was corporate worship which as Stott shows would have taken a number of hours. But, furthermore, there is an emphasis (as indicated in the preceding quote from Origen) on devoting the whole day to holy exercises. Origen's mentor, Clement of Alexandria (*ca.* 150-215) wrote:

> Woman and man (probably 'wife and husband') are to go to church, decently attired, with natural step, embracing silence, possessing unfeigned love, pure in body, pure in heart, fit to pray to God .... But now I know not how people change their fashions and manners with the place .... So, laying aside the inspiration of the assembly, after their departure from it, they

---

21. *Ibid.*, p. 72. Earlier Stott deals with a difficult passage in Clement of Alexandria in which Stott believes Clement refers to the eighth day as the fulfilment of the fourth commandment and calls it the Sabbath, 'And it (the eighth day) properly the Sabbath, the rest, and the seventh (day of the week) a day of work,' p.68.
22 *Ibid.*, 70.

become like others with whom they associate ... after having paid reverence to the discourse about God they leave within (the church) what they heard. And outside they foolishly amuse themselves with impious playing and amatory quavering, occupied with flute-playing and dancing and intoxication and all kinds of trash.[23]

Earlier the writer of the *Second Epistle of Clement* (120-140) called his readers to a faithful observance of the day:

And let us not merely seem to believe and pay attention now, while we are being exhorted by the Elders, but also when we have gone home let us remember the commandments of the Lord, and let us not be dragged aside by worldly lusts, but let us try to come here more frequently, and to make progress in the commands of the Lord ...[24]

The importance of spending the whole day was an emphasis that was retained throughout the remainder of this period. For example, Chrysostom, discussing the dangers of losing the spiritual benefits of the day, says in his commentary on Matthew:

For we ought not, as soon as we retire from the Communion, to plunge into affairs ... unsuitable to the Communion, but as soon as ever we get home to take our Bible into our hands and call our wife and children to join us in putting together what we have heard and then, not before, engage in the business of life .... When you retire from the Communion, you must account nothing more necessary, than that you should put together the things that have been said to you. Yes, for it were the utmost folly, while we give up five or six days to the business of life, not to bestow on spiritual things so much as one day or rather

---

23. Clement of Alexandria, *The Instructor* III.XI.
24. *Second Clement*, XVII. Dated c. AD 120-140.

not so much as a small part of one day ... Therefore let us
write it down as an unalterable law for ourselves, for our wives
and for our children, to give up this one day of the week entire
to hearing and to the recollection of the things which we have
heard.[25]

Commenting on 1 Corinthians 16:2 he calls for the separation of the whole day:

> [O]n the first day of the week ... the separation from all work;
> the soul becomes more joyful from this laying of it aside ....
> Because of this it is fitting that we honor it with a spiritual
> honor ... and every Lord's day let the affairs connected with us
> as masters be laid aside at home.[26]

Stott points out that the early Church also used Sunday for
works of charity, baptisms, ordinations, and church discipline.[27] Thus, though most did not immediately relate the
Lord's day worship to the Fourth Commandment, the early
Church believed that the day of worship and rest had been
changed to the first day and came to think of this day as the
Sabbath. They taught that the whole day should be set aside
for public and private worship and service.

By the fifth century, the Church was firmly committed to
this high view of the Sabbath. The Fifth Church Council of
Carthage (401) decreed that no plays might be performed on
Sundays and petitioned the emperor 'that public shows might
be transferred from the Christian Sunday ... to some other
days of the week ....'[28]

---

25. Chrysostom, *Commentary on Matthew,* Homily 5:1. By 'business of life' he
is not referring to worldly occupations but the necessary work of the household.
26. Quoted in Beckwith and Stott, p. 135. For references to other Fathers such as
Augustine, see Stott and Lee.
27. *Ibid.*, pp. 99-102.
28. Lee, p. 248.

The sanctity of Sunday received great impetus from the decree of the Emperor Leo in 469:

> We ordain, according to the true meaning of the Holy Ghost, and of the apostles thereby directed, that on the sacred day wherein our own integrity was restored, all do rest and cease from labour; that neither husbandmen nor others on that day, put their hand to forbidden work. For if the Jews did so much reverence their Sabbaths, which were but a shadow of ours, are not we which inhabit the light and truth of grace, bound to honour that day which the Lord Himself hath honoured, and hath therein delivered us from dishonour and from death? Are we not bound to keep it singular and inviolable, well contenting ourselves with so liberal a grant of the rest, and not encroaching upon that one day which God hath chosen to His own honour? Were it not reckless neglect of religion to make that very day common, and to think we may do with it as with the rest?[29]

In addition to the Sabbath, however, the Church began to hold other festive days and saints' days. This resulted in a legalistic observance of the Lord's day and eventually a decline in the sanctity of the Sabbath.[30]

The Mediaeval Church

By the sixth century, a legalism with respect to Sabbath-keeping had begun to develop. By 544 physical penalties were prescribed for Sabbath-breaking – a slave was to receive a hundred stripes and a free man to be imprisoned.[31] By 585 the Council of Macon decreed, '"under divine inspiration" that "the implacable anger of the clergy" would be meted out to a Sabbath desecrator, be he "a farmer or a slave", by severe "blows of the lash"; and which ecclesias-

---

29. *Ibid.*, p. 249. 30. *Ibid.*, p. 249. 31. *Ibid.*, p. 249.

tical decision was recommended and enforced by the full power of the state ...'[32]

Although there were intermittent attempts to alleviate this legalism, the Church moved incrementally in the direction of a Judaistical Sabbath with severe penalties. Paradoxically, there was a simultaneous decline in Sabbath-keeping:

> For Sunday services, although well attended, were often poorly led and hardly heeded by the worshippers. This is perhaps not surprising, for the Church had become worldly. It had compromised its position by extending the use of its premises for folk-dancing, games, banquets, sports, buffoonery, festivals, fairs and markets, and consequentially even the Christian Sunday had become a day of exuberant revelry for some and remained a day of labour for others, both of which parties thus desecrated the Sabbath in their own particular way.[33]

Up to the twelfth century, Sunday law was based on the Fourth Commandment, but with the work of Peter Lombard (*ca.* 1110-1160) a dual approach to the Fourth Commandment began to develop. He taught that there was both a literal interpretation of the Fourth Commandment (the Jewish observance of the seventh day) and an allegorical interpretation (the New Testament believer resting from sin). By referring to the pattern of one day in seven as a Jewish observance and emphasizing the allegorical meaning, he severed the day of observance from its Fourth Commandment foundation and opened the door to the doctrine that the church had the authority to select the day.

In his decretals, Pope Gregory IX (1227-1241) claimed that, although Lord's day observance was derived from both the Old and New Testaments, the Pope had the authority to

---

32. *Ibid.*, p. 249. 33. *Ibid.*, p. 251.

appoint Sunday as well as other holy days.[34]

This shift of the basis and authority on which day is to be observed by the Church came to a head in Thomas Aquinas (1225-1274). He taught that the seventh-day Sabbath was Mosaic and thus typical, and that Sunday Sabbath was moral, emphasizing the accomplished work of Christ and resting from sin. He based the authority for Sunday observance on the decision of the Church and custom.[35] Though his position did teach that there remains a moral obligation for the day of rest in the Fourth Commandment and that Sunday replaced Saturday as the Christian Sabbath, he removed the warrant of the Fourth Commandment for one day in seven and the New Testament's authority regarding the specific day that is to be observed. Thomas's position became the official policy of the Roman church and was codified at the Council of Trent.[36] This position also influenced some of the early Reformers.

The Mediaeval church combined a strange mixture of legalistic, superstitious practices with flagrant abuses of the day. Holy days, including Sunday, became holidays. James Dennison says of the Mediaeval Church in England: 'The populace was so enamoured of Sunday sports that the church soon capitulated to the secular spirit and the churchyard became the local fairground ....'[37] Because the Church reserved to itself the authority to select the day, Dennison points out: 'The end result of the Roman doctrine was that the New Testament Sabbath had no authority from God whatever; the Lord's day was grounded in the authority of the church hierarchy.'[38]

---

34. *Ibid.*, 251. 35. Dennison, p. 3. Cf. Lee, 252.
36. Dennison., p. 3.
37. *Ibid.*, p. 2. 38. *Ibid.*, p. 4.

The Reformation Church

The teaching of the early Reformers on the Lord's day and its relation to the Sabbath is a tangled web. Many are quick to point out that the early Reformers repudiated the Sabbath and the principle of one day in seven as Judaistic. Indeed, as we saw in Chapter 7, both Luther and Calvin failed to relate the Lord's day to the one day in seven required by the Fourth Commandment.

The early Lutheran conviction is stated in the Augsburg Confession:

> Those who consider the appointment of Sunday in place of the Sabbath as a necessary institution are very much mistaken, for the Holy Scriptures have abrogated the Sabbath and teach that after the revelation of the Gospel all ceremonies of the old law may be omitted. Nevertheless, because it was necessary to appoint a certain day so that the people might know when they ought to assemble, the Christian church appointed Sunday for this purpose, and it was the more inclined and pleased to do this in order that the people might have an example of Christian liberty and might know that the keeping neither of the Sabbath nor of any other day is necessary.[39]

Luther, however, did teach that the first day of the week was the most appropriate day to observe. Patrick Fairbairn quotes Luther from his German annotations on the Fourth Commandment:

> Although the Sabbath is now abolished, and the conscience is free from it, it is still good, and even necessary, that men should keep a particular day in the week for the sake of the word of God, in which they are to meditate, hear, and learn, for all can not command every day; and nature also requires that one day

---

39. *Augsburg Confession*, Article XVIII.

in the week should be kept quiet, without labour either for man or beast.[40]

In his *Table Talk*, Luther said the apostles alone had the authority to change the day: 'the apostles transferred Sabbath to Sunday, (as) none else would have dared to do it.'[41] Five years before his death he wrote: 'If heretofore I in my discourses spoke and wrote so harshly against the law, it was because the Christian Church was overwhelmed with superstitions under which Christ was altogether hidden ...; but as to the law itself, I never rejected it.'[42] In fact, Luther believed that the main features of the Sabbath observance 'were of universal and perpetual obligation.'[43]

One segment of the Reformed Church (in contrast to the Lutheran Church) believed, like Calvin, that the seventh-day was part of the ceremonial aspect of the Fourth Commandment. Fairbairn says:

> Considering the sabbatical rest, therefore, of every seventh day as a shadow of Gospel realities, they conceived that the moral obligation couched under the figure could be carried no further than to impose the necessity of setting apart such times as might be sufficient to maintain the worship of God; but that it did not strictly bind Christians to confine themselves to one day in seven, as if to take more would be to err in excess or to take fewer would be to err by deficiency. The exact length of the period which was to separate one day of rest from another, under the Christian dispensation, they held should be determined by other considerations.[44]

---

40. Patrick Fairbairn, *Typology of Scripture*, 2 vols in one (Grand Rapids: Kregel Publications, 1989) II, 452.

41. Lee, pp. 253, 254. 42. *Ibid*., p. 254.

43. *Ibid*., 254. Cf. Luther's *Works*, 5, p.22.

44. Fairbairn, II, p. 451.

This sentiment was reflected in the Helvetic Confession:

> But we do not tolerate here either superstition or the Jewish
> mode of observance. For we do not believe that one day is
> holier than another, or that rest in itself is pleasing to God. We
> keep the Sunday, not the Sabbath, by a voluntary observance.[45]

As seen in this reference, although they thought that the Fourth
Commandment did not compel them to adopt one day in seven,
they believed that because of the resurrection and practice
of the apostolic church, the first day of the week should be
observed. As Fairbairn points out:

> [D]id they therefore question that there should be one in seven?
> Not in the least, for there were considerations enough besides
> to fix that as the proper rotation .... The Reformers, at any
> rate, appear to have had no doubt that the day to be observed
> for holy purposes was to be one in each week, not excepting
> those of them who took the most general view of the moral
> obligation imposed in the Fourth Commandment, feeling them-
> selves drawn to that conclusion by a regard to the other pur-
> poses for which it was given, as well as from the primeval
> character of the ordinance, and the recorded procedure of the
> Apostolic Church in keeping the first day of the week.[46]

The Reformers' treatment of the ceremonial and what they
considered Judaistical observance of the Fourth Commandment, grew out of their reaction to the abuses of the Jewish
Sabbath and the practices of the Roman Catholic Church.
Like the early church fathers, they were rejecting what they
thought was the burdensome rest of the day.

---

45. *Second Helvetic Confession*, ch. XXIV.
46. Fairbairn, II, pp. 451, 452.

But the Reformers undoubtedly did believe that a degree of rigour, an extent of prohibition belonged to the Jewish Sabbath, for which we find no proper warrant in Scripture; and well knowing from New Testament Scripture, that no such yoke was laid upon the Christian Church, they naturally drew the equally unwarranted conclusion, that the strictness of prohibition as to the performance of works requiring labour was somewhat relaxed. In using such language, they still did not mean that ordinary works might be performed on any plea of worldly convenience or pleasure, but such only as were performed by our Lord, – works required for the necessary support or the comfort of men, and some of which at least they conceived to have been interdicted to the Jews, for the purpose of rendering their sabbatical rest more exactly typical of the spiritual rest enjoyed by believers in Christ.[47]

Furthermore, they were reacting to the legalistic ceremonialism of the Roman Church. Again quoting Fairbairn:

The gigantic system of heresy and corruption against which they had to contend, was chiefly distinguished by the multitude of its superstitious rites and ceremonies, and the substitution of an outward attendance upon these for a simple faith in Christ, as the ground of men's acceptance before God. This false method of salvation by works had branched itself out into so many ramifications, and had taken such a powerful hold of the mind of men, that the Reformers were in a manner constrained to speak of all outward observances as in themselves worthless, and not properly required to the salvation of sinners. They represented, in the strongest terms, the inward nature of the kingdom of God, its independence of things in themselves outward and ceremonial, so that no bodily service, merely as such, was incumbent upon Christians as it had been in Judaism, but

---

47. Fairbairn, II, p. 454.

was only to be used as a help for ministering to, or an occasion for exercising the graces of a Christian life.[48]

But, even though they were unclear on the relation of the day to the Fourth Commandment, this group of reformers believed that the day should be kept holy for the purposes of worship and service. Certainly this was Calvin's position:

The Sabbath, should be to us a tower whereon we should mount aloft to contemplate afar the works of God, when we are not occupied nor hindered by any thing besides, from stretching forth all our faculties in considering the gifts and graces which He has bestowed on us. And if we properly apply ourselves to do this on the Sabbath, it is certain that we shall be no strangers to it during the rest of our time and that this meditation shall have so formed our minds, that on Monday, and the other days of the week, we shall abide in the grateful remembrance of our God ... It is for us to dedicate ourselves wholly to God, renouncing ourselves, our feelings, and all our affections; and then, since we have this external ordinance, to act as becomes us, that is *to lay aside our earthly affairs and occupations, so that we may be entirely free* to meditate the works of God, may exercise ourselves in considering the gifts which He has afforded us, and, above all, may apply ourselves to apprehend the grace which He daily offers us in His Gospel, and may be more and more conformed to it. And when we shall have employed the Sabbath in praising and magnifying the name of God, and meditating His works, we must, through the rest of the week, show how we have profited thereby.[49]

Dennison concludes with respect to Calvin's position:

48. *Ibid.*, p. 448.
49. Calvin, 34th sermon on Deuteronomy, qouted in Fairburn, vol. II, p. 455. See John Calvin, *Sermons on Deuteronomy* (Banner of Truth Trust, 1987), p. 205.

[I]t should be apparent that Calvin was far from an Anti-Sabbatarian, even though he does ground the worship on the Lord's day in the need for order in the church rather than in the proportion of one in seven found in the fourth commandment.[50]

Others among the early Reformers believed, however, that the Fourth Commandment not only was typical of the spiritual rest provided by Christ, but also that it perpetually required the observance of one day in seven. For example, this was the opinion expressed by Beza, writing on Revelation 1:10:

He calls that day *the Lord's*, which Paul names *the first of the week*, 1 Cor. xvi. 2, on which day it appears that even then the Christians were accustomed to hold their own regular meetings, as the Jews were wont to meet in the synagogue on the Sabbath, for the purpose of showing that the Fourth Commandment, concerning the sanctification of every seventh day, was ceremonial, *as far as it respected the particular day of rest and the legal services*; but that as regards the worship of God, it was a precept of the moral law, which is perpetual and unchanging during the present life. That day of rest had stood, indeed, from the creation of the world to the resurrection of our Lord, which being as another creation of a new spiritual world (according to the language of the prophets), was made the occasion (the Holy Spirit, beyond doubt, directing the apostles) for assuming, instead of the Sabbath of the former age, or the seventh day, the first day of this world, on which, not the corporeal and corruptible light created on the first day of the old world, but this heavenly and eternal light, hath shone upon us.[51]

---

50. Dennison, 6. For a more thorough examination of the views of Calvin and other Reformers see Fairbairn, II, pp. 461-476 and Richard Gaffin, Jr.'s thesis, *Calvin and the Sabbath* (Westminster Theological Seminary, 1962). Gaffin's work will be published by Christian Focus in 1998.
51. Quoted in Fairbairn, II, pp. 452, 453.

This was the opinion, as well, of Viret, a colleague of Calvin's in Geneva:

> Since we have from God every thing we possess, soul, body, and outward estate, we ought never to do any thing else all our lives, than what He requires and demands of us for the true and entire sanctification of the day of rest. Nevertheless, we see that He assigns and permits us six days for doing our own business, and of the seven He reserves for Himself only one – as if He had contented Himself with the seventh part of the time which was specially given up and consecrated to Him, and that all the rest was to be ours .... What ingratitude is it, if in yielding us six parts of the seven which we owe Him, we do not at the least strive with all our power to surrender the other part, which He exacts of us, as a token of our fidelity and homage! .... Since we are permitted all other days of the week excepting this for attending to our bodily concerns, it seems to me that we hold very cheap the service of God and the ministry of the Church, on which we ought to wait more diligently on that day than any other, if we can not find means for employing one whole day of the week in things which God requires of us upon it. For they are of such weight and consequence that we must take care, in every manner possible, lest we occupy ourselves with any things which might turn our attention elsewhere; so that we may not bring our hearts by halves, but that ourselves and all our family may without distraction apply.[52]

Bullinger in Zurich also held that the observance of the Lord's day was based on the Fourth Commandment. Commenting on Matthew 12, he says:

---

52. Quoted in Fairbairn, II, p. 456. Cf. Bucer in the fifteenth chapter of his work on the kingdom of Christ.

Sabbath signifies rest, and is taken for that day which was consecrated to rest. But the observance of that rest was always famous and of highest antiquity, not invented and brought forth for the first time by Moses when he introduced the law; for in the Decalogue it is said, 'Remember the Sabbath-day to keep it holy', thereby admonishing them that it was of ancient institution.[53]

This was the view held by the German and Dutch Reformed Churches, as well. Some interpret the Heidelberg Catechism as being 'looser' on the Sabbath than *The Westminster Confession*. In answering question 103, 'What doth God require in the fourth commandment?' The Heidelberg Catechism teaches:

First, that the ministry of the gospel and the schools be maintained; and that I, especially on the Sabbath, that is, on the day of rest, diligently frequent the Church of God, to hear His word, to use the sacraments, publicly to call upon the *Lord*, and contribute to the relief of the poor, as becomes a Christian. Secondly, that all the days of my life I cease from my evil works, and yield myself to the Lord, to work by His Holy Spirit in me, and thus begin in this life the eternal Sabbath.[54]

Some claim, on the basis of this answer, that although the Fourth Commandment requires public worship, its New Testament fulfilment is primarily typical, pointing to our rest in Christ. Note, however, that the Catechism uses the term 'Sabbath' for the Church's appointed day of worship on the first of the week.

Moreover, Ursinus (one of the framers of the Heidelberg Catechism) says in his commentary on the Catechism that the

---

53. Quoted in Fairburn, II, p. 449
54. *The Heidelberg Catechism*

Commandment has two parts: 'the *one* moral and perpetual, as that the Sabbath be kept holy; the *other* ceremonial and temporary, as that the seventh day be kept holy.'[55]

With respect to the moral duties he writes:

> God allots six days for labour, the seventh He claims for divine worship; not that He would teach that the worship of God and meditation upon divine things is to be omitted on all other days beside the Sabbath, but, 1. That there might not only be a private worship of God on the Sabbath as at other times, but that public worship might also be observed in the church. 2. That all those other works which men ordinarily perform on the other days of the week, might on the Sabbath give place to the private and public worship of God.[56]

This is essentially the position adopted by the Dutch members of the Synod of Dordt in a resolution designed to settle the Sabbath controversy in Holland:

> 1. In the Fourth Commandment there is something ceremonial and something moral;
>
> 2. The ceremonial was the rest of the seventh day, not the rigid observance of that day prescribed to the Jewish people;
>
> 3. But the moral is, that a certain and stated day was appointed for the worship of God, and such rest as is necessary for the worship of God, and devout meditation upon Him;
>
> 4. The Sabbath of the Jews having been abrogated, the Lord's day must be solemnly sanctified by Christians;
>
> 5. From the time of the apostles, this day was always observed in the ancient Catholic Church;

---

55. Zacharias Ursinus. *The commentary of Dr. Zacharias Ursinus on the Heidelberg Catechism.* (Phillipsburg, N.J.: Presbyterian and Reformed Publishing Company) 557.

56. *Ibid.*, 558.

6. The day must be so consecrated to divine worship, that there shall be a cessation from all servile works, excepting those which are done on account of some present necessity, and from such recreations as are discordant with the worship of God.[57]

In Holland, Gomarus, and later Cocceius, advocated the position that the Fourth Commandment was purely ceremonial. Since their views were contrary to the Synod of Dordt, they caused great dissension in the Church. Although they were ably refuted by Voetius and others, much damage was done.[58]

In God's providence, the English Puritans of the sixteenth and seventeenth centuries brought together the conflicting strands of Reformational thinking on the Sabbath to give us the 'English Sabbath'. The Puritans clarified and refined the thinking of the English Reformers, who reflected the ambiguity of the early Reformers on the Continent. Fairbairn quotes Archbishop Whately 'that the English Reformers were almost unanimous in disconnecting the obligations regarding the keeping of the Lord's day among Christians from the Fourth Commandment, and resting it simply on the practice of the apostles and the early church – thus making the Christian Lord's day an essentially different institution from the Jewish Sabbath.'[59] The position of the early English Reformers is summarized by Cranmer:

But we Christian men in the New Testament are not bound to such commandments of Moses' laws concerning differences of times, days and meats, but have liberty and freedom to use other days for our Sabbath days, therein to hear the word of

57. Quoted in Fairbairn II, p. 448.
58. Lee, pp. 261-264.
59. Fairbairn, p. 122.

God and to keep an holy rest. And therefore that this Christian liberty may be kept and maintained, we now keep no more the Sabbath or Saturday as the Jews do, but we observe the Sunday and certain other days, as the magistrates do judge it convenient whom in this thing we ought to obey.[60]

Two of the English Reformers who escaped the confusion were the proto-Puritan, John Hooper, and Hugh Latimer. Hooper taught that Sunday was the Christian Sabbath: 'This Sunday that we observe is not the commandment of man ... but it is by express words commanded, that we should observe this day for our Sabbath, as the words of St. Paul declareth, 1 Cor. xvi ...'[61]

Moreover, although most of the English reformers were confused over the relation of the Lord's day to the Fourth Commandment, they advocated a strict observance of the day. Dennison summarizes their position:

(1) a significant protest against the abuse of Sunday and other holy days; (2) civil and ecclesiastical statutes enjoining spiritual duties on the Lord's day; (3) Sabbath sanctification promoted by church and state for the sake of worship and order in the establishment; (4) identification of the Sabbath of the fourth commandment with a day, the observance of which is binding upon Christians; (5) a theological distinction between spiritual and external Sabbath; (6) a litany which requires worshippers to beseech God for the inclination to keep the Sabbath commandment.[62]

---

60. Dennison, 8. Spelling modernized by me. For a thorough discussion of the pre-Elizabethan reformers see Dennison pp.1-13.

61. John Hooper. *Early Writings of John Hooper,* ed. for the Parker Society by Samuel Carr (Cambridge, 1843), 342. Cf. Latimer in Hugh Latimer. *Sermons by Hugh Latimer,* ed. for the Parker Society by George Elwes Corrie (Cambridge, 1844), 471-473.

62. Dennison, p. 13.

Thus, although the English Reformers mistakenly believed that the specific day could be set by church and state, they held that the moral part of the Fourth Commandment remained binding.

The Puritans had the opportunity to reflect on the conflicting thoughts of Calvin and their own English fathers and to work out exegetically the position that is encapsulated in *The Westminster Confession of Faith* and explained in this book.

They established the distinction of moral-positive law to demonstrate that the moral requirement of the Fourth Commandment is to observe one whole day in seven as the Sabbath. Before Christ that day was the seventh day and after the Resurrection the first. As Dennison observes:

> Strict logic would compel the obvious development (against the background of the Puritan principle of hermeneutics, i.e. the sole and explicit testimony of Scripture in matters ecclesiastical) – a day for divine service free from profane distractions must have its ground in something more substantial than apostolic succession and tradition ...[63]

Following the Puritans, the uniform practice of English and Scottish Reformed churches until the middle of this century has been the Sabbatarianism of the Westminster Standards. Such was also the practice of English and American Baptists and Methodists. In Holland, although there was more theological resistance, the primary position favoured a strict observance of the Lord's Day.[64]

But in the second half of the twentieth century the decline of the biblical doctrine of the Sabbath has been widespread.

---

63. *Ibid.*, p. 15.
64. Lee, 264, 265.

Today Reformed Christians are compromising on the Sabbath, returning to arguments that have been consistently repudiated throughout the history of the Church. While on paper most Reformed denominations remain committed to the doctrine of Sabbath-keeping, in the church courts and in the teaching and preaching of a growing number of Presbyterian and Reformed pastors, its glorious truth and privileges are being denied. Again the park is overgrown and desolate. May God see fit in these days to restore the park for the sake of His Church.

10

THE WORK OF THE SABBATH

I have endeavoured to demonstrate that the observance of the Sabbath or Lord's day is a continuing New Testament ordinance, morally binding on all people. The park is not a historic site to be preserved as a museum piece, nor is it to be sacrificed to the desires of modernism. God has appointed the park as a place for special transactions with Him – the market place of the soul. He promises to meet with and bless those who seek Him in its ordinances. I also have sought to demonstrate that though the use of the park remains the same, the day of the transactions has been changed. God moved it from the seventh day to the first day of the week. Furthermore, although church history is not an infallible interpreter, it confirms that a commitment to the Lord's day has been predominant in the church until the past few decades.

In the remaining chapters I want to concentrate on how to use the day, beginning by examining the crowning work of the day.

Celebrating God and His works in corporate worship
The most important thing you will do on the Lord's day is join with God's people in corporate worship. Psalm 92 looks at corporate worship and its relation to the Sabbath. From its title, we note that this psalm is 'a song for the Sabbath Day'. The titles of the Psalms relate to us either the historical background and circumstances of the Psalms or some-

thing of their usage. For centuries, the Church has used this psalm to guide her in her Sabbath work.

We will focus on the corporate work of the congregation. Of course, what we do in corporate worship carries over into the other activities of the day, so we will learn something of the purpose of the day, as well.

Psalm 92 teaches that God has appointed the Sabbath as a day for the work of celebration, anticipation, and re-creation. The psalmist begins in verses 1-4 with the work of celebration:

> It is good to give thanks to the LORD,
> And to sing praises to Thy name, O Most High;
> To declare Thy lovingkindness in the morning,
> And Thy faithfulness by night,
> With the ten-stringed lute, and with the harp;
> With resounding music upon the lyre.
> For Thou, O LORD, hast made me glad by what Thou hast
> > done,
> I will sing for joy at the works of Thy hands.

I use 'celebration' not in the narrow sense of the festival activity of God's people, but to embrace the glorious activity of exuberantly praising God. The psalmist calls us to worship and honour God. Although we serve God in all of life, the crowning act of service is the corporate worship of the church. The Lord's day is a special time to give thanks to the Lord, to sing praises to His name, to declare His lovingkindness and faithfulness, to sing for joy at the works of His hands. In corporate worship, we speak and sing to Him of His excellence, declaring His name in our fellowship to one another as well as to non-Christians who visit our worship service. As a part of that declaration we give thanks to the Lord by remembering corporately His mercies to us, by reflecting on the good and generous care that He provides for us. He takes great pleasure in our worship; in fact, He saved us for this purpose (John 4:21-24). The Sabbath gives us the opportunity to devote ourselves to this great work.

The psalmist teaches that our worship springs out of a profound realization of who God is and what He does. In verse 1, the psalmist directs our attention to two of God's names. He instructs us to offer our praise to God as 'LORD' (Yahweh), the self-sufficient, eternal God, who loves His people with covenant love. Furthermore, he calls us to give thanks to 'God Most High' (El Elyon), the sovereign possessor of heaven and earth (Gen. 14:19). We are to worship God as sovereign Creator and Ruler, and as our personal Saviour. Thus, we who are bought with a price (1 Cor. 6:20) have a double responsibility to praise God: we praise Him because He is a sovereign Master who made and owns us, and we give thanks to Him as our covenantal Saviour.

In addition to His names, God's attributes or personal characteristics increase our understanding of who He is. In verse 2, the psalmist directs us to declare God's lovingkindness in the morning and His faithfulness by night. The psalmist selects these two attributes – lovingkindness and faithfulness – to represent all of God's attributes. He chose these two as manifestations of the names 'LORD' and 'God Most High'. Surely, it is appropriate to give special consideration to the Lord's covenant love and mercy as we begin a day. His lovingkindness is His covenantal love: the mercy and grace He bestows on us for Christ's sake. Beginning the day by reflecting on God's covenantal love sets the tone for the entire day. You are a child of God, having been elected, redeemed, justified, and adopted on the basis of sovereign grace.

Moreover, what better way to close a day than by reflecting on the faithfulness of God Most High? His faithfulness is His unswerving commitment to His word. Everything He has said in His word, He will do. He keeps every promise. He fulfils every threat. He keeps covenant with us. He is always trustworthy. At the conclusion of the day as you are about to fall asleep, you look back at His faithfulness. He has sustained you. He has heard your prayers. He has done for you all that He promised and infinitely more.[1]

By exalting these two characteristics, the psalmist directs our attention to all of God's attributes. These two are windows into the world of God's character. Thus, the psalmist reminds us that we should focus on God's attributes every day in order to love Him and proclaim His name. But the Lord's day with its corporate worship should be the climax of our daily reflection and praise. Sunday itself, in its memorial of the resurrection of Christ, is a beautiful reminder of God's covenantal love and His faithfulness in providing full salvation for His people. When we gather on the first day of the week, we declare His attributes in our songs, prayers, offerings, readings, sermons, and sacraments. God has given us this day to turn aside from our work and activities of the other six days and join with the covenant community in the declaration of His goodness to us. When we do

---

1. Some have suggested that the reference to morning and evening point to the necessity of having two worship services on the Lord's day. As suggestive as this is, we probably cannot make an airtight case on the basis of this language, though the pattern does match that of the morning and evening sacrifices. The chief practical reason for two corporate services is that corporate worship is the primary means of grace, and by following the pattern of the Old Covenant, the church wisely gives the people of God two occasions to worship the Father and to enjoy the means of grace (Cf. *The Larger Catechism* 154, 155).

this God is glorified, and we are encouraged and built up in the faith (Heb. 10:24, 25).

The psalmist also leads us to praise God for His works: 'For Thou, O LORD, hast made me glad by what Thou hast done, I will sing for joy at the works of Thy hands' (verse 4). God has appointed the Sabbath to remind us of the twin works of creation and redemption. The Lord's day and its worship is a prism through which the light of God's glory is revealed. The glorious work of the Saviour is seen in its many faceted splendour: 'This is the day which the LORD has made; Let us rejoice and be glad in it' (Psalm 118:24). By His rest on the seventh day, God declared creation was complete and under the government of His providence. He invites us to rest under His Lordship and rule. By the Saviour's rest on the first day, God declared the work of redemption complete and that all authority in heaven and earth belong to Christ in order that He may gather and perfect His elect (Matt. 28:18; Eph. 1:22, 23). The Sabbath focuses our attention on these great works, and corporate worship gives us the opportunity to serve as God's choir, singing psalms and hymns that celebrate the great works of God.

Our worship is not only directed to the great works of God in history, but also to His works of providence and redemption in our particular lives. We should often reflect upon and talk about His ways with us in saving us, keeping us, leading us through or by His Word, hearing our prayers, etc. Such reflection gives a personal element to our praise and service. Therefore, our great Sabbath work is to join with the Church in the public acts of worship that praise His name and give thanks for who He is and what He does. The reading and preaching of the Word interpret the great deeds of God and teach us His will so that we may know how to respond.

The last phrase of verses 4, 'I will sing for joy at the works of Thy hands,' teaches us the attitude that should colour our worship. When we properly reflect on God and His work, we will gather on the Lord's day with an attitude of exuberant joy. Notice how the psalmist begins the psalm, 'It is good to give thanks' (verse 1). He reminds us that corporate worship is pleasant and beautiful. We then should come with the enthusiasm of a sports fan to celebrate the glories of our God.

The psalmist does not approach worship nonchalantly. Rather, he approaches worship with enthusiasm and longing. Joy and exuberance fill his heart as he comes to do the work, and he accentuates his exuberance by his reference in verse 3 to the various musical instruments. Although we cannot with any certainty identify many of these instruments, we know they were part of Levitical worship in the temple. Calvin says that these instruments are types of the beautiful, glorious Saviour who was to come. Commenting on this passage, he points out:

> We are not to conceive that God enjoined the harp as feeling a delight like ourselves in mere melody of sounds; but the Jews, who were yet under age, were astricted (*sic*) to the use of such childish elements. The intention of them was to stimulate the worshippers (*sic*), and stir them up more actively to the celebration of the praise of God with the heart.[2]

Thus, our great Sabbath work is celebrating God and His works in corporate worship. We are not just to go through the set forms and traditions. No, our whole being should vibrate with the beauty and glory of God, as we declare His

---

2. John Calvin. *Commentary on the Book of Psalms*, 5 vols. (Grand Rapids: Eerdmans) III, 495.

loving-kindness and faithfulness. As we are made glad by His works, we speak to one another and together declare the glory and excellency of these works.

To worship in this manner, however, we need to come prepared. Worship is sometimes meaningless and dull because we approach it totally unprepared. Because we have not spent any time glorying in the presence of God, our affections are unstirred. We come with cold hearts, depending on the social activity of corporate worship to warm our hearts and to make us ready, whereas, we ought to approach worship like a racehorse, straining, longing to begin the race. We should come to worship having been already in God's presence through meditation and prayerful preparation.

The necessity of preparation highlights the importance of having a day dedicated to this work. If we are to devote ourselves to exuberant praise of God, we must be free from other distractions. God has given us a day free from distractions to study and reflect upon His works and to declare His name. When we recognize God's wisdom in clearing away the distractions of work and recreation, we will resent those things that hinder our worship. I find it impossible to believe that one can rush from work to worship and from worship to play, and fulfil the glorious work of corporate celebration.

When I plan a special time with my family, I am jealous for that time. A few years ago, we bought an answering machine to screen calls, because whenever we tried to have family time, we were interrupted by unnecessary phone calls. I did not want to have to think about work or to talk to some salesperson while I was trying to spend time with my family. Similarly, with the Lord's day, I want to give my attention to God and His wonderful works. If I am thinking about business, talking about a ball game, or catching up on the news, I cannot concentrate on God the way I should.

Therefore, the purpose of avoiding recreation and work is so we can be made glad by the person and work of God through study, meditation and worship. God gives us the Sabbath to free us for this glorious work of corporate worship, the great work of the Sabbath. Celebration of God is the first work of the Sabbath.

Anticipating the eternal rest

The second aspect of the Sabbath and its worship is anticipation. Because Sabbath-keeping points to our eternal Sabbath rest, the Sabbath and its worship enables us to look beyond our present strife to heaven. A perennial problem for the Christian is the prosperity of the wicked and the persistent afflictions of the believer. Why do the wicked so often go unscathed, while the righteous limp through life? For the psalmist, the Sabbath with its worship enables us to place things in perspective. Here we may get a clearer picture of the ways of God. The Lord's day towers like a mountain over the landscape of our present existence; from its heights, we have an eternal perspective. I have hiked a number of 14,000 feet mountain peaks in the Colorado Rockies. The views are phenomenal, and how different the landscape looks from that vantage point! So the Sabbath's view of life is very different.

We saw in a previous chapter that a Sabbath-keeping remains for the people of God, because the day with its worship reminds us that, although we have begun to participate in eternal rest, the full rest with its victory is yet to come (Heb. 4:9-11). Thus, the Sabbath and its worship point to the solution of the problem of the prosperity of the

wicked and the troubles of the righteous by setting the reality
of eternity and judgment before our minds. We see the wisdom
and greatness of the ways of God (Rom. 11:33-36). The
Sabbath enables us to rise above all of the pressures, the
attacks, and persecutions of life, as we anticipate Christ's
return.

The Sabbath perspective reminds us that God is the om-
niscient, righteous judge whose judgment is inevitable. In
light of this, the psalmist reflects on the end of the wicked.
The wicked wallows in his prosperity, taking no thought of
eternity. He cannot see beyond the nose at the end of his
face. In truth he is like a beast: 'A senseless man has no
knowledge; Nor does a stupid man understand ...' The word
translated senseless is 'brutish'. The natural man is no better than a beast. He is the worldling who lives in the midst
of prosperity, and his vision is obscured by the very prosperity that he enjoys. In his spiritual stupidity, he never looks
beyond today's pleasures. Samuel Johnson compared the
brutish man to a bull in the pasture: 'If a bull could speak, he
might as well exclaim, – Here am I with this cow and this
grass; what being can enjoy better felicity?'[3] The very prosperity that God has given to him to elicit his grateful attention becomes an end in itself that blinds him to God (Acts
14:17).

He fails to grasp the fact that his life and all his pleasures
and prosperity are here today and gone tomorrow:

That when the wicked sprouted up like grass,
And all who did iniquity flourished,
It *was only* that they might be destroyed forevermore
                                                    (Psalm 92:7).

---

3. Quoted in Derek Kidner, *Psalms 73-150* (London: IVP, 1975) p. 335.

They are green and flourishing like the grass or the herbs of the field. But what happens to grass? It eventually dies; it is cut to be composted, or fed to cows. Like grass, the prosperity of the wicked is green and lush, but ephemeral. Like hay, the wicked flourish only to be cut down. If they do not respond to God's blessing by repentance and faith, they will harden their hearts and continue their blind rush into hell. Their ingratitude will be fodder for God's righteous anger.

By contrast, the righteous know that God is sovereign and will judge with equity. The Sabbath reminds us that God is sovereign and will exercise judgment in due time:

> But Thou O LORD, art on high forever.
> For, behold, Thine enemies, O LORD,
> For, behold, Thine enemies will perish;
> All who do iniquity will be scattered   (Psalm 92: 8, 9).

Because God is on the throne, regardless of what we see in this world, His enemies will perish. Judgment is coming. Although we will not see the full execution of His judgment in this life, Christ will come as judge and put an end to this godless world and all those who have lived in rebellion against Him. We wait like the saints under the altar in Revelation 6:9 who cry out, 'Lord, when will You vindicate the blood of Your church?' and are told 'not yet, but in My time'.

Now this is what the Sabbath with its activities, particularly with its corporate worship, does for us. The Sabbath gives us an eternal perspective as it is the pledge of our eternal rest and vindication. It helps us look at life from a totally different vantage point so that we no longer measure things by our present circumstances but are taught to measure things by the character of God and His eternal justice.

We are reminded that there is a day appointed for man to die and after that the judgment (Heb. 9:27).

Further, the Sabbath enables us to do this not only by being the pledge of our eternal rest, but also reminding us that God has accomplished victory in Christ. As noted earlier, we keep the Sabbath on the first day of the week because of the resurrection. Christ's resurrection was His vindication and guarantees not only our justification (Rom. 4:25), but also our resurrection (1 Cor. 15: 20, 21).

The psalmist anticipates the vindication of the Messiah in verses 10 and 11:

> But Thou has exalted my horn like *that of* the wild ox.
> I have been anointed with fresh oil.
> And my eye has looked *exultantly* at my foes.
> My ears hear the evil doers who rise up against me.

The psalmist speaks not only of himself, but also of the Messiah. In this psalm, Christ is depicted in His suffering, the one who was humiliated and cast down, despised and rejected of men. He lived His life in poverty and rejection; the one truly righteous man did not prosper. The crowning ignominy was His cruel death on the cross in which both men and God cursed Him. In His death, the wicked seemed to prosper; apparently their judgment of Him was correct, since God did not deliver Him from their hands.

But His confidence was that His horn would be exalted. The figure of a horn is used in the Psalms to picture might and strength. The horn of the wild ox is a figure of strength, of victory and majesty. God promises that the crushed one, who was trampled by the feet of men and Satan, would rise up in majesty and power. He would be rewarded in His righteousness with a refreshing anointing. The oil of joy makes

Him more glad than His fellows (Psalm 45:7). 'The stone which the builders rejected has become the chief corner stone. This is the LORD's doing; it is marvelous in our eyes' (Psalm 118:22, 23). Yes, He was beaten down; He was a man of sorrows; the unrighteous seemed to prevail, but His horn was exalted. He was freshly anointed by the Spirit when He was raised from the dead. In His resurrection, He looked exultantly upon His foes and heard of their judgment: all those who continue in rebellion against Him would be damned (Psalm 2:7-12).

As we celebrate Christ's resurrection on the first day of the week, we get the eternal perspective. By His resurrection, God reminds us that, though we go through the valley of the shadow of death, we shall be victorious in Him. God has appointed that, like Him, we enter glory through tribulation. The God who raised Him from the dead shall raise us as well. He shall say, 'Well done, good and faithful servant.' The Sabbath with its corporate worship reminds us of these truths.

On this mountain top of the Lord's day, with its corporate worship, we can stand above life's difficulties. We can have a different perspective, a different focus on life. We can anticipate eternity with its joys and with the justice and vindication of God. In Psalm 73 the psalmist testifies to the reality of this work. He had envied the wicked and was tempted to deny God, but he says in verses 15-19:

> If I had said, 'I will speak thus,'
> Behold, I should have betrayed the generation of Thy children.
> When I pondered to understand this,
> It was troublesome in my sight
> Until I came into the sanctuary of God;
> *Then* I perceived their end.

Surely Thou dost set them in slippery places;
Thou dost cast them down to destruction.
How they are destroyed in a moment!
They are utterly swept away by sudden terrors!

In the sanctuary, in the midst of God's worship, he climbed up on the mountain and saw things as God sees them. This is the second work of the Sabbath, the work of anticipation.

The Lord's day with its worship directs our attention to God and eternity. How we need this. We need to get away from the toil and dayliness of living and be reminded that a better day is coming. This not only fortifies us in suffering and persecution, but also arms us against worldliness. Spiritually, we need adjustments, and if we cling to our worldly tasks and recreations on the Lord's day, we will not be realigned with God's perspective, and the world will tighten its grip on us. Again we see God's wisdom in giving us the gift of the day – the park.

The work of re-creation
The third work of the day, in addition to celebration and anticipation, is 're-creation'. Verses 12 to 15 of Psalm 92 say:

The righteous man will flourish like the palm tree,
He will grow like a cedar in Lebanon.
Planted in the house of the LORD,
They will flourish in the courts of our God.
They will still yield fruit in old age;
They shall be full of sap and very green,
To declare that the LORD is upright;
He *is* my rock, and there is no unrighteousness in Him.

Notice the contrast between verse 7 and verse 12. The prosperity of the wicked is compared to grass that flourishes today and is gone tomorrow. In contrast, the prosperity of the righteous is compared to a palm tree and a cedar, trees known for their beauty, long life, usefulness, and fruitfulness.

The tall, stately palm tree is a figure of long-lived beauty and fruitfulness. I have read that palm trees can live over 200 years and often bear fruit for 40 to 100 years. The temples of Solomon and Ezekiel were decorated with engraved palm trees (2 Chron. 3:5; Ezek. 41:18-20) as symbols of eternal life and fruitfulness.

The cedars of Lebanon are large, aromatic, dome-shaped trees, with long branches and evergreen foliage. Like California Redwoods and Sequoias, they can live for centuries. Some have grown to be 63 feet in girth and over 70 feet tall. The Bible often uses them as symbols for strength and majesty (Ezek. 31:3-9).

By these figures, the psalmist reminds us that the righteous are like trees planted by water, constantly bearing fruit (Ps. 1:3). Their spiritual vitality shall not be diminished by age; they will still yield fruit in old age, remaining full of sap and very green (verse 14). In fact, often, as the body decays and the senses fail, the soul becomes all the more alert and attuned to the beauties of God and the glories of heaven. Verse 15 brings us back full circle, saying, they 'declare that the LORD is upright; He is my rock, and there is no unrighteousness in Him.' The very presence of the elderly in the corporate assembly shall declare the lovingkindness and faithfulness of God.

Now how does this relate to the Sabbath? Notice the righteous are planted in the sanctuary, 'Planted in the house of the

LORD, they will flourish in the courts of our God' (verse 13).
They are fruitful and long-lived because they dwell in the
presence of God. Since this psalm is about the Sabbath and
its worship, we rightly infer that they are nourished in the
corporate worship of the Sabbath day. Again we are reminded
of the promise of Isaiah 58:13, 14:

> If because of the Sabbath, you turn your foot
> From doing your *own* pleasure on My holy day,
> And call the Sabbath a delight, the holy *day* of the LORD
>   honorable,
> And shall honor it, desisting from your *own* ways,
> From seeking your *own* pleasure,
> And speaking *your own* word,
> Then you will take delight in the LORD,
> And I will make you ride on the heights of the earth;
> And I will feed you *with* the heritage of Jacob your father,
> For the mouth of the LORD has spoken.

Thus the true recreation of the Sabbath is not found in the
games, entertainment, and pleasures of this present life. We
are to cease from these things in order to seek the pleasures
of knowing the Lord. Ordinary recreation on the Sabbath
will rob you of the true re-creation promised. As you are
under the means of grace, in the midst of God's people and
in the presence of the Lord Jesus Christ, you will flourish.

So the work of the Sabbath day, particularly viewed as a
corporate work, is a work of celebration, anticipation, and
re-creation. Note the interesting parallel between these three
things and God's rest on the seventh day. His rest was a
cessation from His particular work of creation, while our
rest is the cessation from our weekly labours so that we may
be recreated in the observance of the Sabbath. His rest was

a joyful contemplation of His work, while ours is the celebration of the great deeds of God. His rest promised eternal life, while ours is the anticipation of the glory that is to come.

May each of us be zealous for this work. May we seek to guard our lives and the lives of our children so that we may enjoy these benefits of the Sabbath day.

Even though corporate worship is the chief work of the Sabbath, it is not the exclusive work. The market day of the soul is marked by the assembly, but also personal dealings with God and labours in His service. In the next chapter, we will consider the private duties of the day.

11

PRIVATE DUTIES OF THE SABBATH

Have you ever had 'cabin fever'? During the time I wrote this book, we had an extraordinarily severe winter in the United States and in Europe, with much more snow than usual. Many people have been snowed in, some for days. Some of us enjoy being snowed in, but others develop 'cabin fever'. They come to the point that, if they have to stay inside for one more day, they will go crazy. They need to be physically active. Or perhaps others of you have wrestled with having to spend time with people who were virtual strangers. The thought of a mandatory day with distant relatives fills you with dread. What in the world will you do? What will you talk about? I am afraid the boredom of 'cabin fever' and the dread of an afternoon with virtual strangers mark the attitude some of us have toward our use of the Sabbath day.

When we read in *The Larger Catechism* that we are to 'make it our delight to spend the whole time (except so much of it as is to be taken up in works of necessity and mercy) in the public and private exercises of God's worship,'[1] panic sets in. How do I fill up a day without television, work and play? What in the world do I do with my children? The purpose of this and the next chapter is to give you some practical suggestions as answers to these questions.

In the previous chapter, we looked at the work and privileges of corporate worship. If your congregation has two

---

1. *The Larger Catechism* 117.

worship services and Sunday school, you might spend four to six hours at church. You still have ten to twelve hours in the day. What do you do? What are these 'private exercises of God's worship'?

Using the time meaningfully

Of course, there are the necessary duties connected with the day. Some meal preparation and clean-up and a certain amount of housework will be necessary. When there are not older children to help, I recommend that the husband help with the kitchen chores, particularly cleaning up after the meal. This frees the wife to rest from what is part of her normal vocation.[2] If you properly prepare for the Lord's day, there will be fewer household chores to be done on Sunday.[3]

Nevertheless, after having done the necessary chores, you may still have seven to nine hours. How do you use this time meaningfully? First, take time to review the sermon.[4] Although a sermon, as the powerful word of God, has an immediate effect, it also works like a time-release capsule. We will benefit from it during the week if we mull it over by meditation and discussion. You will be amazed how much more you will remember when you use this type of review.

This should be done as soon as is convenient. In our home

---

2. In homes where there are older children they should be trained at taking turns with household chores. In the household where both husband and wife work outside the home (before children are born or after they leave home) there should be an equitable division of household chores.

3. In Chapter 12 we will deal with removing as many of these things as possible.

4. Note the practical advice of *The Larger Catechism*, 160, 'What is required of those who hear the word preached?' 'It is required of those that hear the word preached, that they attend upon it with diligence, preparation, and prayer; examine what they hear by the Scriptures; receive the truth with faith, love, meekness, and readiness of mind, as the word of God; *meditate, and confer of it; hide it in their hearts, and bring forth the fruit of it in their lives*'(emphasis mine).

we discuss the sermon during or at the end of our meal. Some families might have a sermon review and then family worship, while others combine the two things.

Review the sermon by discussing the main points and purpose of the sermon. Review the main headings of the outline. What does the text mean? Are there things you did not understand? Parents should help their children to fill in the gaps of understanding. Ponder the application, personally appropriating the message. Were there any sins mentioned you ought to deal with? Duties to obey? Promises and comforts to believe? Judgments threatened? How was your faith encouraged to receive and rest on Christ alone for justification and sanctification? In family prayer, confess sins and seek grace for comfort and duty.[5]

The time after the mid-day meal may be used for extended family worship; perhaps, as well, a special time for the family to spend in singing and praying. During the week, times for family worship suffer from crowded family schedules. You will find this particularly true, if the father travels in his work or the children have sports and other after-school activities. Sunday is a good day to make up for lost time.

For those of you who do not have children or whose children have grown up, you will still want to take advantage of this extra time to read, discuss, sing and pray together. Family worship is not only for the children; adults profit from this time together, as well.

When family worship is over, the kitchen is clean, and the afternoon stretches out before you, the course of least resistance leads to sleep. As mentioned in Chapter 5, a nap may be a necessity, but we should not spend the entire after-

---

5. These suggestions, in part, are based on the book by Dave Eby, *Power Preaching* (Inverness: Christian Focus Publications, 1996). See Appendix.

noon asleep. In this chapter, we will focus on things you and older children may do to use the day profitably.

Just as family worship often suffers during the week, your private times with the Lord probably suffer more. Sunday is God's gift, a day for you to do some of those things you do not have as much time for during the week. As noted earlier, the Lord's day is like a spiritual vacation. When I go on vacation, I like to take along a stack of books that I have not had time to read. God gives you leisure on Sunday to complete your Bible reading for the week and to study. Perhaps you have used a Bible-reading calendar, but every year you fall behind and give up. You may use Sunday to catch up and keep on track.

Moreover, you will have the same time constraints during the week with respect to private prayer; often your prayer-time is rushed, perhaps because of the children's needs and so on. The Lord's day afternoon gives you extra time for prayer.

Sunday also affords you time for more in-depth study of a book of the Bible or a particular doctrinal theme. If you teach a Bible study or Sunday school class, Sunday offers you an opportunity for preparation of that week's lesson. (Such study, on Sunday, does not rule out review during the week, particularly before you teach.)

Sunday afternoon is also a good time to review memory work. As Christians, we ought to be memorizing the Bible and Catechisms systematically. In our congregation, we work through *The Shorter Catechism* every three years. We also memorize assigned portions of Scripture and emphasize that the success of any memorization programme depends on frequent review. Sunday is a great time for this.

If you are like me, you have a stack of unread Christian

magazines and periodicals, Sunday is a wonderful time to catch up on this type of reading. Personally, I find Sunday night, when I am more tired, to be a good time for the lighter reading of magazines.

But, in addition to unread magazines, there are books you need to be reading. We all should have some kind of reading programme, alternating books on Christian experience (prayer, communion with God, etc.), biography, and doctrine. None should take refuge in the excuse of not being a reader. Each of us can and should develop reading skills and habits, and a reading plan. Ask your pastor or elder to help you develop such a plan. Sunday afternoon gives you an opportune time to read systematically.

Using the time for hospitality

The above are a few suggestions for private activities on the Lord's Day. But the day is also profitably spent in Christian fellowship. Hospitality is a requirement for all Christians (Heb. 13:2; Rom. 12:13; and 1 Pet. 4:9). A Sunday meal is a great time to have guests into your home for fellowship. The scope of your hospitality may include the needy (either the poor or someone in town over the weekend, staying in a hotel), friends from the congregation, and visitors to church services.

The very word 'hospitality' scares the wits out of some people, for whom it conjures up pictures of an elegant meal set off by elaborate place settings. True, some people (like my wife) enjoy preparing such a meal for guests. It is her way of saying, 'You are special.' Usually much of the meal preparation can be done the day before. But true hospitality does not suggest nor require an elaborate meal. Hospitality

6. See suggested reading lists on pages 245-6.

is sharing what you have with someone else – anything from a special meal, to each person fixing his own sandwich, to sharing left-overs. Whether you eat in the dining room on fine china or in the family room off paper plates, the key ingredient is not where or what you eat, but making people feel comfortable and welcome, and creating an environment for spiritual conversation.

Spiritual conversation is the key ingredient to biblical hospitality. This is nearly a lost art, yet one greatly used by God in the lives of His people.

By such conversation we share needs for prayer and encouragement, talk about things we are learning from the Bible, converse about the ways of God in our lives, and encourage and exhort one another. We all need to train ourselves in the art of spiritual conversation. The exercise of hospitality is a good way to learn. As we develop our ability in this area, we will be able to avoid unnecessary conversation about work and play.

The course of the conversation will be dictated by the guests and your purposes in inviting them. If you are entertaining them for the mid-day meal, you ought to continue with your regular family worship and sermon review. This practice in itself will help set a direction for conversation.

At times you will not know your guests. Then you will want to learn about them, their family, and their work. If they are Christians, you want to learn about God's work in each other's lives. If they are not Christians, direct the conversation as much as possible to a testimony of God's work in your life, or sharing the gospel with them.

Sometimes you will invite people for specific purposes, such as to discuss a problem or to seek or give counsel. Other times you will invite Christian friends, to spend time with each other and promote holiness in one another (Heb. 10:24, 25). Friends may be like those unread books and magazines: the business of the week and family get in the way of developing intimate relationships. So Sunday is a great time to spend with Christian friends for the purpose of spiritual conversation.

God Himself takes great pleasure in these times of Christian conversation:

> Then those who feared the LORD *spoke to one another*, and the LORD gave attention and heard it, and a book of remembrance was written before Him for those who fear the LORD and who esteem His name. 'And they will be Mine,' says the LORD of hosts, 'on the day that I prepare My own possession, and I will spare them as a man spares his own son who serves him.' So you will again distinguish between the righteous and the wicked, between one who serves God and one who does not serve Him (Mal. 3:16-18).

Here the prophet mentions the practice of the righteous (those who feared the LORD and esteemed His name) speaking with one another. By contrasting verse 16 with 13-15, we infer that they were vindicating God's name and encouraging one another in holiness. The Lord paid close attention to these conversations, taking note of them to reward them. In response He vindicated His people and caused them to stand out in their holiness.

It is important that you schedule times for hospitality. Some fall into a pattern of inviting people over every Sunday. When you do this, other important activities of Sabbath-keeping will suffer and the duties of hospitality may become burdensome, especially for wives. A good schedule is a monthly mid-day meal on Sunday and one or two Sunday evening meals.

When we exercise hospitality on Sunday, we need to be careful not to neglect our children or leave young ones to fend for themselves. Be creative with the children and provide opportunities for their fellowship and edification as well.

Using the time for ministry

Churches may also have special opportunities for fellowship on Sundays. Our church has a mid-day meal on the first Sunday of each month and an evening meal on the third Sunday. We use these times (especially the evening) for various activities. Once a quarter, we schedule our ministry team meetings.[7] By doing this we avoid unnecessarily taking people out of their homes during the week. On the other two Sundays of the quarter we may have a missionary speaker or a special presentation from the officers or a ministry team, but most often we have a 'Christian experience' meeting. The purpose of this meeting is to discuss questions about the sermons or other theological or practical issues. The emphasis is on the experimental nature of the truth. How does it work itself out in the believer's experience?

Furthermore, you may profitably use Sunday afternoon or evening for ministry. Earlier, we discussed the practice of doing deeds of mercy on the Lord's day. Emergency situations will arise, but you may also plan regular visits to the elderly and ill. Perhaps your church has planned activities in which you could participate: witnessing in public places, rescue missions, prison ministries, nursing home visits, etc. Or, you could visit people who are ill or lonely.

---

7. This is the name we use for Sessional and Diaconal committees. By referring to them as ministry teams we avoid the business model and help promote a biblically based ministry model in the church.

Our church does door-to-door evangelism on Sunday. In our case we send out teams during the Sunday school hour, which is 11 am. The teams rotate so that no-one is out of Sunday school more than once a quarter. This time of day is ideal, since the non-churched are up but usually still at home. Other churches, however, do the same thing on Sunday afternoons or after the evening service.

Sunday afternoon or evening may be a good time to encourage elders to do family visits. Many churches encourage their elders to exercise a pastoral oversight and participate in family visitation. Some conscientious elders get frustrated because they cannot seem to fit one or two visits a month into their schedules. Why not schedule one on a Sunday afternoon or evening? Surely the purposes of such a visit actively promote the purposes of the day.

Sundays are good times to do discipleship as well. In our congregation, both individuals and couples are involved in discipling other individuals or couples. New Christians or those new to the Reformed faith are given a basic introduction to the faith. Mature couples do premarital counselling or marriage counselling to prepare couples for marriage or to help couples who are having marriage difficulties. Other couples who have exhibited faithfulness and wisdom in raising children help prepare others for the birth of their first child. All of these activities may be incorporated into regular patterns of using the Lord's day with profit.

Where is the rest?
By now your fears about how to spend the day have surely evaporated, perhaps to be replaced by a new fear, 'Where is the rest?' First, remember the rest of the Lord's day is not a rest of inactivity. It is a spiritual rest of meditation, study,

fellowship, service and worship as well as a cessation from daily labours. Such a rest will give vigour to body and soul. However, the activities of the Lord's day should not leave us exhausted or spiritually unrefreshed on Monday. Do not become involved in so many activities of fellowship or service that you neglect private and family duties and activities.

Furthermore, remember that Sabbath-keeping does not rule out taking some physical rest. Sometimes people object to the Catechism's interpretation of the Fourth Commandment because they think it prohibits physical rest when it says, 'making it our delight to spend the whole time (except so much of it as is to be taken up in works of necessity and mercy) in the public and private exercise of God's worship.'[8] This instruction does not rule out taking a nap. As we have already noted, the warning of the Catechism is against sleeping most of the afternoon and thus neglecting private devotion or service.

The same may be said about physical activity. In the next chapter, we will discuss the necessity of some form of physical activity for our children. Some adults, as well, may need a walk in order to be refreshed and alert for evening worship. Such a walk may well be used for meditation or review of memory work. Lewis Bayly wrote:

1. Walk into the fields and meditate upon the works of God; for in every creature thou mayest read, as in an open book, the wisdom, power, providence, and goodness of Almighty God (Psalms 92:5; 19:1ff.; 8:1, 3ff.; Rom. 1:19, 20); and that none is able to make all these things in the variety of their forms, virtues, beauties, life, motions, and qualities, but our most glorious God (Isa. 40:26).

---

8. *The Larger Catechism* 117.

2. Consider how gracious He is that made all these things to serve us (Psalm 8).

3. Take occasion hereby to stir up both thyself and others to admire and adore His power, wisdom, and goodness; and to think what ungrateful wretches we are, if we will not, in all obedience, serve and honour Him.[9]

If you walk with others such as your children, you may spend the time profitably in spiritual conversation.

A further way to avoid fatigue is by planning your day. Have goals for the day; know what you will do. Plan time for service and hospitality around the completion of certain books, memory work, time with the children, etc. Never fill the day with so much that you have no time for quiet reflection.

Pastors

Perhaps a word is in order to Pastors. Admittedly your Lord's day will be somewhat different, but you may enjoy the private duties as well. Some pastors have no time for family or private duties on Sunday afternoon, because they are busy with the evening sermon. Thus, other than in the privilege of corporate worship, their day is little different from their other work days. Some pastors compensate by taking a Sabbath rest on some other day in addition to a day off. I question this solution for a couple of reasons.

First, you have the privilege most work days of spending much more time in the Word and reading than the people you serve. What a glorious privilege it is to work daily with the Scriptures! Second, if you manage your work well, you will not need Sunday afternoon to prepare. In fact, I doubt that

---

9. Lewis Bayly, *The Practice of Piety* (Morgan, PA: Soli Deo Gloria) 201, 202.

such preparation is a proper use of the Sabbath. Have your sermons completed, so that you have time for your wife and children on the Lord's day.

So, the faithful believer need not fear cabin fever. When you keep the Lord's day with purpose, it will be that wonderful means of grace promised in Isaiah 58:14.

In the next chapter, we will look at making the day a delight for our children.

12

MAKE IT A DELIGHT

On more than one occasion, when I have taught on the beauty of the Lord's day, I have been approached afterwards by a person who said that, having been raised in a home that strictly observed the Christian Sabbath, he would never submit his children to such torture. As I enquired about the practices of his home, I learned that Sunday observance consisted of morning and evening church services, family worship, and a list of things the children could not do. For these children Sunday was only a form of dreary punishment.

If we want our children to love the Sabbath, we must make the day a delight for them. As we have seen, there are activities that are not to be done on the Lord's day and, as parents, we must teach our children not to pursue such things. But our instruction must not dwell on the negative; we need to teach our children the wonderful things that they may do on the Lord's day. For little ones this entails doing things with them and providing special Sunday activities for them.

The things I mention here are but suggestions which I have gleaned from books, conversations with friends, and our own family practice.

Regular teaching of children
You lay a foundation for making the Sabbath a delight for your children by regularly teaching them the principles involved. As you explain other rules from the Scripture to

your children, teach them and review with them the importance and use of the Lord's day. Help them to see that God
commands them not to do their regular daily activities so
that they may devote themselves to Him. Also use your
instruction about the Sabbath to remind them of the
importance of resting in Christ alone for their salvation.
Relate Sabbath observance to faith and love for God. Teach
them, therefore, that the motive for doing or not doing certain
things is to please God and to have more time for His worship
and service.

Since I deal with preparation for the Sabbath in the next
chapter, in this chapter I will concentrate on the positive
activities of the day. A positive view of Sabbath-keeping
for children begins by instructing them about the privileges
of corporate worship and training them how to worship. I
believe that children should be with their parents in the public worship services. For a time, somewhere from 6 to 24
months, depending on the child, it might be difficult for children to be in corporate worship. Their physical development during this time makes it difficult for them to sit quietly
in one place. But once they develop the ability to sit still and
be quiet, they should be in the public assembly.[1]

If we believe that in corporate worship we come into
God's presence in a unique way and that preaching is the

---

1. A great diversity of opinion exist on this issue. Some churches have Sunday
school during worship for young children, while others have 'Children's Church'.
Others have a 'Children's Sermon'. Jay Adams defends the practice of sending
children out of the worship service in *Shepherding the Flock* 3 vols. (Grand
Rapids: Baker Book House, 1976) III, 119. He cites Nehemiah 8:2 to prove that
the congregation consisted of 'men and women, and all that could hear with understanding'. In contrast, however, there are countless references to children and
babes in arm as part of the worshipping assembly (Deut. 31:12, 13; 2 Chron.
20:13; 31:18; Ex. 10:1, 2; Neh. 12:43).

primary means of grace[2] because in it we hear the living voice of Christ, we will resist depriving our children of this privilege. If Christ were on the earth and you had the choice of letting your children hear Him teach or go off to Children's Church, what would you choose? The answer should be obvious. I once asked the same question to a five year old girl; her face lit up as she said, 'I would want to stay with Jesus.' The Triune God is present in our worship and Jesus Christ speaks uniquely in the preaching of His Word. Why deprive our children of these inestimable benefits by sending them off to Children's Church?

Sunday School Catechism Classes are important, supplementary instruction. These activities are adapted to the age characteristics of the children and assist the parents in laying the foundation of Christian nurture. Corporate worship, though, with preaching, is for the entire covenant community. Particularly, those of us who believe that our children are under Christ's Covenant Headship and have that sealed to them in baptism, should include them in the assembly of the covenant people at worship.

If then, we are to include them, we need to teach them how to worship. We must instruct them in what we do in worship and why. We ought to help them memorize the Creeds, the Lord's Prayer, the Ten Commandments and other items that are used in our services. In the church my family attends, the children are taught a new psalm or hymn each month (alternating a psalm one month and a hymn the next). We attempt to use these psalms and hymns in our weekly worship.

Furthermore, we should teach our children how to listen to a sermon. When they are very young, we might draw a

2. *The Larger Catechism* 155.

picture for them that illustrates an important truth in the sermon. Later they can draw their own pictures and then learn to take notes, first writing down in portant words they hear, then eventually learning to take notes in an outline form.[3]

The preacher should keep in mind that little ones are present and use illustrations and make some points or applications that are aimed at them. Every child can learn something from a sermon. Once I was asked why I did not give Children's Sermons.[4] After explaining my theology of preaching, I asked the father, 'How many things would your child get from a children's sermon?' 'One point, of course,' he answered. I asked, 'Can he not get one truth from my sermon, especially if you go over that point with him afterwards?' Therefore, both preacher and parent have the responsibility to be sure the child learns something from the sermon.

Teach children how to behave in church
We can also train our children to sit through the service. Often we take our children out of the service, because we do not want to spend the energy to train them to sit and worship. We may do a number of things as officers, parents, and members to help train children. One specific way to help children is to get them settled down before the service begins. It has been observed that the more the children run and play before the worship service, the more difficult it is for them to settle down. Little ones cannot change gears as quickly as

---

3. Some question the use of note taking in sermons. Each person should do that which best enables him to listen. For some note taking is a distraction while for others it enables them to concentrate. For our children though it is a good tool to train them how to listen. Some will outgrow it while others will make it a lifetime habit.

4. It is my conviction that when a lawfully ordained man preaches, Christ Himself speaks in a unique way; the act of preaching is a divine, supernatural act, and a child's object lesson is not preaching.

adults can. Furthermore, parents should not worry about fidgeting and wiggling. Such activity is normal and usually worries the parents more than it distracts others around them. Those of us who have older children or no children in the worship service need to be patient with the little ones. We ought to rejoice that God has given so many children and encourage the parents to bring them into the worship service.

Families with young children should also choose carefully where to sit. Because they might have to get up and leave during the service and since children fidget, parents often feel it is best to sit in the back. Yet, when children sit closer to the front, it is easier for them to pay attention.

But what if the child insists on misbehaving or talking in the service? It is recommended that a parent take the child out, discipline him and bring him back in. At times, children will push their parents for as long as they think they will get away with their disobedience. In public situations like the worship service, they often think they have freedom to misbehave because parents would be embarrassed to take them out for correction. When they realize that they will be disciplined, they often will be more obedient. What about taking them into the nursery when they disobey? This does not help at all. When they realize that bad behaviour gets them into the nursery, they will seek to manipulate parents to that end.

Much at this point depends on your general patterns of discipline. When parents consistently teach their child that they mean what they say and will consistently punish him if he does not obey, he will be more inclined to heed the whispered correction during the worship service.

Children in the home

Having discussed children in the worship service, let us now turn our attention to the rest of the day. We might be at church for five to six hours, but our children will be up another eight to ten hours. What do we do with them the remainder of the day?

The noon and evening meal are good times for sermon review. Our children will profit from preaching and develop their skills as sermon listeners as we review the sermon with them. Help the little ones to concentrate on an important truth from the sermon and how they may apply it in their lives. As they grow older, review the outline with them, and discuss the main points and the application. You may also use the dinner hour to discuss with them what they learned in Sunday School. Review that material with them to cement it in their minds. Later in the day look over the assignments for next week and help them to prepare for that lesson.

The conclusion of the noon meal on Sunday is an excellent time for extended family devotions, which compensate for abbreviated family worship during the week. You have more time on Sunday to spend in Bible reading and discussion. As children learn to read, they love to take a turn in reading the Bible story or Scripture portion. This aids their memory and develops early skill in Bible reading. Subsequent discussion helps them to develop the skills of biblical analysis and application. Sunday also provides more time to spend in prayer, so that all may participate in family prayer. Sunday devotions are a good time as well to devote to family hymn singing: singing favourites, learning new hymns and psalms, singing the hymns and psalms that were used in the morning worship, and practising those that will be used in the evening service.

In connection with family devotions little children often enjoy acting out a Bible story.[5] We kept a box of Bible character dress-up clothes, which encouraged our children to review creatively the Bible stories. (Our children's favourite was David and Goliath.)

Children may also enjoy preparing music for the family and guests. They can prepare programmes similar to what they do for special fellowships at the church, in which they combine songs and Scripture and catechism recitation. Older children can help younger ones put together such a programme. When two or three families get together for the Lord's day, this can be a joint exercise of the older and younger children.

Sunday afternoons are good times for Scriptural and catechetical memorization and instruction. Remember, it is primarily the parents' responsibility and not the church's to teach covenant children. Many churches have memorization goals. If your church does not, then plan your own.[6] Little children have a love and facility for memorization. Take advantage of this God-created aspect of their development to help them memorize Scripture and the Catechism. As soon as they can talk, begin with the Children's Catechism and then go to the Shorter or the Heidelberg Catechism.

Be creative in helping them memorize. You can use games and songs.[7] When our son was about three he loved to build

5. I believe that drama in the corporate worship is not acceptable to God. But such prohibitions do not rule out the place for plays and skits in the life of the covenant community. In the same way a fellowship meal is an important part of the life of the church but is not a part of the corporate worship.

6. If you would like a copy of the catechism programme used at our church, Trinity Presbyterian Church in America, write to me care of the publishers.

7. Judy Rogers has put a number of catechism questions and answers to song on a cassette tape, 'Why Can't I See God?'. You may order this tape from Judy Rogers, P.O. Box 888442, Atlanta, GA., 30338

log cabins with a toy building set called 'Lincoln Logs'. On Sunday afternoon we would build a log-cabin mission school and he would teach the make-believe children in the school house the Catechism. He quickly memorized the Catechism and indirectly learned the importance of foreign missions.

You may make creative use of toys in helping your little children learn to keep the Sabbath. Some families keep a box of Sunday toys. This box could contain the dress-up clothes mentioned above plus other Sunday games and activities. What you want to avoid is merely playing. Rather, strive for playing with a purpose: playing to learn and review or playing to create values or attitudes. A number of games are available that are very good learning tools.

Your little children will need a great deal of supervision if they are to profit from the Sabbath and learn its beauty. You will need to resist the temptation to use games as 'baby sitters' so you can go about your own activities, remembering that as they mature they will increasingly be able to do more on their own.

Little children can profit, as well, by the use of videos. Some very good videos are available for Sunday use: various Bible stories, *Pilgrim's Progress*, and *The Chronicles of Narnia*, to name a few, are available. But do not allow the use of videos to replace your involvement with your children on Sunday afternoons.

One of the best ways to spend time with your children on Sundays is reading to them, although reading aloud is a good family activity any time. Have a family circle in which you read a story together. Even when children are older and can read for themselves, reading aloud as a family is much more profitable than watching a video and creates wonderful memories. Take time on Sunday afternoons or before bed-

time Sunday night to read to your children. Again a wide
range of profitable books are available: missionary stories,
biographies, and Christian adventure stories. One pastor
friend speaks fondly of his father's reading the *Pilgrim's
Progress* to the family every Sunday evening. Older children may also read to their younger brothers and sisters.
Such an activity builds greater bonds among them and helps
the older children develop the attitude of servants.

As you build your family library, select books for your
children. As they learn to read encourage them in their reading
on Sundays. By this they will develop good habits and learn
to keep the Lord's day holy. Early on, foster the habit of
reading biographies and missionary stories. This type of reading will promote good role models and engender a concern
for the spread of the gospel. As they grow older, introduce
them to doctrinal and devotional reading, so that they will
develop a taste for books that are more expositional and
didactical.

A needful, but much neglected activity is to discuss with
your children the ways of God in your life and what He is
doing in their lives. Children love to know about your past;
tell them the stories of how God brought you to Himself. If
you come from a Christian home tell them of God's work in
the lives of their grandparents and great grandparents. Use
the family picture album as a way to make the stories live
for them.

Speak to them as well of God's providences in your life:
how 'mommy' and 'daddy' met and married; how God has
provided for physical and financial needs; how you came to
live where you live and do the kind of work that you do. As
they grow older relate to them the struggles and temptations
you went through when you were their age: what mistakes

you made and what lessons God taught you, that they might learn from your experience.

Learn to speak intimately and personally to them of God, His beauty and wonderful ways. Use this time as well to enquire of the Lord's work in their hearts. Asking not only about their love for Jesus, but also what He means to them, how He affects their choices and desires. Are their affections for the Lord developing? Do they enjoy prayer, Bible reading, and worship? What are their struggles? Get them to think and talk about God's work in their lives.

Sunday evening before going to bed is an excellent time for these discussions.[8] You can pull together the threads of the day's activities and help your children get the fruit of the day and apply it to their hearts. If you spend regular time discussing the ways of the Lord with your children when they are young, it is not likely they will have difficulty talking to you about personal things when they are teenagers.

Also involve your children and young people in Christian service. Take your children with you to visit the elderly who are unable to get out of their homes or are in a nursing home. This activity will breed compassion in your children and a desire to serve others. The elderly usually delight in the presence of children. My own first taste of ministry was going with a woman in our congregation to visit the elderly in their homes. She would have me read Scripture and pray. Churches that have Junior or Senior High youth groups should help them organize activities for Christian service and evangelism. Older youth can conduct devotional services in

---

8. Of course, these conversations will not be limited to Sunday. We want to develop the facility of spiritual conversation all the time. But as with Bible reading and other activities, we will have more leisure for these types of conversations on the Lord's day.

nursing homes, rescue missions, and centres for men and women in the armed services.

Many of the youth activities in our churches fall prey to the hedonism current in our culture, so young people think primarily of having a good time. It is good for our Christian young people to have fun together, but they must also learn to serve and minister. The church in which I became a Christian has been used by God to put more men in ministry than any church with which I am familiar, because, in my opinion, as teenagers we were actively involved in ministry projects. Through these projects God gave us a heart for ministry and enabled us to begin identifying and developing our gifts. Furthermore, great spiritual good was accomplished.

At this point a word about physical activity is in order. Most little children are very active. Sunday can become oppressive if they do not have outlets for their energy, so some families allow their children to run and play for a while in the yard in order to expend some of this energy. When our children were little we would get on the floor and tumble and wrestle. But in addition, you may lead them in a number of creative activities that combine the expenditure of energy with the purposes of Sabbath-keeping.

We already mentioned the ideas of skits or musical presentations. Often the planning and execution of these activities gives a sufficient vent for pent-up energy. Instructive walks are helpful. One friend fondly talks about the walks with his parents on the Lord's day afternoons when they would talk about the things that God made. We would take our children on walks and talk about God's creation. You may also use walks to review the Catechism or to talk about God's work in your lives.

Occasionally, you might incorporate these things in Sun-

day afternoon picnics. When we lived in the city of Philadelphia, we would often go to a park on Sunday after church
to escape the noise of the city. After eating, we would have
family devotions and then go for a walk in the park. On these
walks we would do Catechism or talk about things God had
made. We would often play a game with the children pointing out things made by God. Be careful not to allow such
outings to become distractions: you need to avoid places or
situations in which the surroundings turn your attention away
from your intended purpose.

The benefits of making the Sabbath a delight to your children are unparalleled. Not only will they develop a delight
in keeping the Lord's day holy, but also you will see the
promises of Isaiah 58:13, 14 fulfilled in their lives. The spiritual maturity of young people raised in homes in which the
Lord's day was carefully observed often surpasses that of
those from homes that have neglected this privilege. I am not
forgetting that God is sovereign in the conversion and sanctification of our children, but He uses means, and Isaiah 58:13,
14 is a promise for you to claim for your children as you
teach them to keep the Lord's day holy.

Of course, each child will need to own the truth for himself.
Some will turn away for a period, but most will make it
their own practice as they remember its pleasures and benefits.

A practical benefit for young people is in the area of peer
pressure. We all are aware of the immense pressure on
teenagers to conform to the standards of the world. As
Sabbath-keeping puts to death idolatry and self-gratification,
it also helps children learn to live by a standard different
from the world's. Sabbath-keeping will teach them 'Just Say
No!' Early on, a child whose family is committed to joyfully

observing the Lord's day will learn to say no to invitations to go to a party or to play ball. As they grow older, they will have developed the character necessary to resist external pressures. They will be better equipped to walk by God's standard in other areas of life, having learned early on to deny themselves for the Lord's sake.

Sometimes they will also see that they can influence others for the good by taking a stand. I remember when my son Joey was young, a friend invited him to a birthday party on a Sunday afternoon. When my son informed his friend that he could not attend because it was on Sunday, his friend went to his mother and asked to have the party on Saturday so Joey could come. Our children and youth can lead by godly example and character. In addition, who knows how many have been or will be brought to know Jesus Christ as Saviour because a Christian young person said, 'I am sorry, but I cannot do that with you because it is Sunday.'

Of course, it will not always turn out this way. Often our children are deprived of legitimate activities because of our commitment to keeping the Sabbath day holy. I know children who have been unable to participate in special sports and gymnastic activities, because the events were held on Sunday. It hurts. But we have opportunity on these occasions to teach them the privilege and obligation of self-denial. Our children, as well as we, will begin to experience the blessing promised to those who are persecuted for righteousness sake (Matt. 5:10-12).

Make the day a delight. This positive approach to the Lord's day does not guarantee the conversion of our child or that he will grow up loving the Sabbath, but God blesses the means and He will bless those who love and keep His day holy.

13

PLANNING AHEAD

Vacations can be mixed blessings. The preparations can be tedious; if not done, the holiday can be a disaster. For instance, we will need to tie together all the loose ends of business and family responsibilities if we are to be gone from home for a week or more. Bills must be paid ahead of time, and arrangements made for the mail, newspapers, plants and pets. Often on the eve of a vacation, I am up until the early hours of the morning preparing for our absence, but when proper preparations are made, the vacation is a time of genuine relaxation.

If we are to spend our Sabbaths profitably and find delight in them, we need to prepare as well. In discussing the religious life of his parents, R.L. Dabney wrote:

> How sacredly was the Sabbath improved! My father went about making the best of the sacred day just as seriously and systematically as any wise business man planning to put in the best work possible on some favorable day in the middle of harvest. He evidently acted on this clear, rational and conscientious conviction, 'I have a great and urgent work to do for my own soul and others'; the one day in seven which a kind Heavenly Father has endeavored to secure for me, for this task, is none too much, if improved to the best. So I must make the most of it.'[1]

---

1. Johnson, Thomas Cary, *The Life and Letters of Robert Lewis Dabney* (Edinburgh: The Banner of Truth Trust, 1977) 10.

If we approach the Lord's day in this manner, we can expect great blessing from God. In this chapter, we will look at a number of ways to prepare for the Lord's day.

Practical preparations

First, *tie up the loose ends*. Use Saturday to complete the work and domestic responsibilities of the week. Finish your work so you do not have to think about it until Monday morning. Plan to leave time on Saturday to complete whatever chores cannot be done during the week. Some may object that they do not have enough time to get everything done, but remember, God gave you six days to do all your work and pleasure. One wise pastor has said, 'If you cannot complete your work in six days, you have taken on more than God intends.'

Sabbath-keeping promotes stewardship of time in the way tithing promotes stewardship of possessions. Tithing not only teaches that God is the sovereign disposer of all our possessions, it also demands a more careful use of our money, since we will have less to work with. As Sabbath observance sets aside one day for the Lord, it also reminds us that He has given us six days for our work and recreation. When we limit life's regular responsibilities and pleasures to six days, we will necessarily make better use of our time.

Second, *learn to plan ahead*. Be sure your car is serviced. My wife and I learned this lesson the hard way. For the first six years of our marriage, we lived next door to the church building. When we moved to Philadelphia for me to do graduate studies, at first we had to drive a great distance to attend church, and I was not in the habit of checking the fuel gauge on Saturdays. It took two Sundays of not having sufficient gas to drive to the church for me to learn the lesson of preparation. Now, car maintenance is a regular part of our Saturday afternoon checklist.

Develop the same habits with respect to groceries and sundries. Check on Saturday to be sure you have everything you need for Sunday. In this way you are not tempted to buy basics such as bread, milk or soap on Sunday.

Another part of planning ahead on Saturday is to have your clothing for Sunday selected and ready. Determine on Saturday what you and the children will wear on Sunday. How many families arrive late for church or in a foul temper, because when they were ready to go out of the door, one of them could not find one of his dress shoes?

Also plan ahead for your Sunday meal. Some families enjoy a special dinner on Sunday. If the preparation of that meal is put off until Sunday morning, those responsible for it will not be prepared for worship, and Sunday will be like every other day. Try to do all the basic preparation a day or two before so that minimal work is required on Sunday morning.

A third aspect of Saturday preparation is *physical*. Have you noticed that you are often more tired on Sunday than the other days of the week? In our house, we attribute this to the 'adrenaline switch'. If you do not have serious public responsibilities on Sunday, your body will stay more relaxed. You have run hard all week on 'nervous energy', and because you are more relaxed on Sunday, the body's turbo does not switch on. You probably notice the same thing on the first few days of a vacation. Although you may be getting more sleep than usual, you are often listless. In preparing for Sunday, you need to compensate for this phenomenon by getting plenty of rest on Saturday night.

Plan your evening so you will be in bed in time to get your required amount of sleep. Often we treat Saturday night as a free night, thinking we can stay up late because we can sleep later on Sunday. On the contrary, we should be the most careful about our sleep on this night. Even when we get our required 'eight hours' of sleep, if it is not during our normal sleep cycle, we will not be as rested the next day. For example, if you normally sleep 10:30-6:30, but on Saturday night you sleep 12-8:00, chances are you will not feel as rested. And even if you are rested, you will have less time to prepare for worship.

In our house, we try to have everything finished so we can shut down by seven o'clock on Saturday evening. We try to avoid social activities that keep us out past this time. When our children were at home, we preferred them to stay in on Saturday night, or if they had a special activity, to be home by ten. Your family may arrange things differently, but by all means be physically rested for the Lord's day.

Sunday fatigue may be accentuated because we exerted ourselves too much on Saturday. Sometimes we work or play ourselves to exhaustion on Saturday. Just as a young child may become so tired he has difficulty going to sleep, adults can reach a point of fatigue that will cause them not to sleep well. Then on Sunday their system shuts down. Therefore, be moderate in your physical exertion. Know your limits and act accordingly.

These suggestions for Saturday preparation reflect the counsel of *The Larger Catechism*'s answer to the question, 'How is the Sabbath or the Lord's day to be sanctified? And, to that end, we are to prepare our hearts, and with such foresight, diligence, and moderation, to dispose and seasonably dispatch our worldly business, that we may be the more free and fit for the duties of that day.'[2]

---

2. *The Larger Catechism* 117.

In connection with the importance of preparation for the Sabbath, some advocate keeping the Sabbath from Saturday evening until Sunday evening. Theoretically, such a schedule is not improper. The commandment requires a whole day, but does not tell us when the day begins and ends. The Hebrews, of course, ordered their day from sundown to sundown. As you work out your own practice you need to keep two things in mind:

First, the Jewish manner of ordering the day is not divinely mandated. Whether one keeps a day from sundown to sundown or from midnight to midnight is a liberty of culture. The Bible demonstrates this when the apostle John uses the Roman method of reckoning time to describe the events around Christ's crucifixion. In thus accommodating himself to his readers, John shows that there was nothing wrong in keeping time differently from the Jews.

Second, in order to avoid the appearance of evil, it is best to keep the Sabbath according to the manner of reckoning time in our own culture. Therefore, I think it is preferable to keep the day from midnight to midnight.

Spiritual preparation

In addition to physical and mental preparation, let us consider the necessary spiritual preparation for the Lord's day. Some will prefer to do some of these things on Saturday evening, while others will do the majority of their spiritual preparation on Sunday morning. The important thing is that we enter the day with our hearts prepared for the work at hand.

This matter of preparation for the acts of worship is of the utmost importance. In his excellent little book, *A Remedy for Wandering Thoughts in the Worship of God*, the Puritan

Richard Steele warns that lack of preparation is one of the four great causes of being distracted in worship. He wrote:

> The third cause of distractions in the service of God is, unpreparedness unto it. 'If thou prepare thine heart, and stretch out thine hands to Him; if iniquity be in thine hand, put it far away; then shalt thou be stedfast' (Job 11:13-15). First prepare the heart, then stretch out the hands. He that keeps not his foot when he goes into the house or service of God, is very likely to stumble, and to offer but the sacrifice of fools. He that is unfitted for any work, must needs be unfixed in it. As holy Mr. Dod used to say of afflictions, 'When we are prepared for them, they are like a sword that only strikes upon our armour; but when we are unprepared, they are like a sword striking on our bare skin.' Even so, when the heart is well fixed and prepared for the Lord's service, an impertinent thought or suggestion falls on our armour, but when we come unprepared, it meets with our very hearts, and runs away with them. If a man come into a prince's presence undressed, unbrushed, or without his band, you may easily imagine how, when he is aware of the feathers or dirt that is about him, he is distracted; so is the soul wofully carried off when approaching to God; the follies of sin and vanities of the world disfigure and divert it from a close converse with him; and therefore a serious Christian doth not only pray, and watch in prayer, but watcheth unto prayer.[3]

Therefore, the profit of the day and worship depends upon our approach to the day. We should begin the day with *thankfulness for the Lord's day* and its great benefits, reminding ourselves that this is the day appointed to celebrate the resurrection of our Lord and the eternal life that is ours in Him. We begin then by faith, reminding ourselves that Christ alone

---

3. Richard Steele. *A Remedy for Wandering Thoughts in the Worship of God* (Harrisonburg, VA: Sprinkle Publications, 1988) 72, 73.

is our hope and salvation. Only as we are resting in Him can we begin to observe His Sabbath rest in a fitting way. We rise with the words of Calvin's hymn:

I greet thee, who my sure Redeemer art,
my only trust and Saviour of my heart,
who pain didst undergo for my poor sake;
I pray thee from our hearts all cares to take.

Next, *spend time in self-examination*. By using the Ten Commandments, the Sermon on the Mount, or some other ethical portion of Scripture, examine your life in order to discover and confess your sin. Such an exercise is particularly necessary in preparation for the Lord's Supper, but is always advantageous.

An outline for this self-examination is given in *The Larger Catechism*:

Q. How are they that receive the sacrament of the Lord's Supper to prepare themselves before they come unto it?

A. They that receive the sacrament of the Lord's Supper are, before they come, to prepare themselves thereunto, by examining themselves of their being in Christ, of their sins and wants; of the truth and measure of their knowledge, faith, repentance; love to God and the brethren, charity to all men, forgiving those that have done them wrong; of their desires after Christ, and of their new obedience; and by renewing the exercise of these graces, by serious meditation, and fervent prayer.

We examine ourselves by the Word of God to discover our sins and weaknesses, to test the reality of our faith and to evaluate our love for God and men. This work then leads us to Christ. Biblical self-examination will always lead us to

Christ – both His completed work of redemption and His on-going intercessory prayer. Moreover, we will have fresh reasons for gratitude as we approach corporate worship. We will also be stirred up to make use of the public means of grace.[4] We will approach corporate worship with a sense of need, but also gratitude for pardon, longing for grace, and a passion for praise.

Moreover, if we enter into corporate worship with un-confessed sin, we are in danger of quenching and grieving the Holy Spirit (Eph. 4:30; 1 Thess. 5:19). Christ warns us in Matthew 5:23-26 that we must deal with sin before we come to worship:

> If therefore you are presenting your offering at the altar, and there remember that your brother has something against you, leave your offering there before the altar, and go your way; first be reconciled to your brother, and then come and present your offering. Make friends quickly with your opponent at law while you are with him on the way, in order that your opponent may not deliver you to the judge, and the judge to the officer, and you be thrown into prison. Truly I say to you, you shall not come out of there, until you have paid up the last cent.

Remember as well the warning of Psalm 66:18: 'If I regard wickedness in my heart, the LORD will not hear.' Thus, if our worship is to be profitable, we approach God through self-examination and confession.

---

4. *The Larger Catechism* 154: 'What are the outward means whereby Christ communicates to us the benefits of His mediation?'

'The outward and ordinary means whereby Christ communicates to His church the benefits of His mediation, are all His ordinances; especially the word, sacraments, and prayer; all which are made effectual to the elect for their salvation.'

A third aspect of spiritual preparation is *to seek to stir up your affections* so that you attend church ready to adore and praise God. We were reminded in Chapter 10 that our worship is to be exuberant. If we are to enjoy worship, we must enjoy God. We enjoy God by thinking on Him as He has revealed himself to us in His names, attributes, and works. On Sunday mornings spend some time meditating on the character and work of God, until your affections are actively engaged. Some families will sing psalms and hymns to help stir up their affections. Others play cassettes or CDs of psalms and hymns in the morning as the family prepares or in the car as they drive to worship.

A fourth part of preparation is *to seek God earnestly in prayer for His aid to us and the congregation in worship*. We should be in prayer during the week for the pastor as he prepares, that God will give him a message for the people of God. We know that if God does not open the Scriptures to the pastor, there will not be a word for us. Additionally, we should pray that God will prepare our hearts and minds for the message. Furthermore, we ought, as well, to be in prayer during the week for the proclamation of the Word, that the pastor will preach in the power of the Holy Spirit. In our more immediate preparation for the Lord's day we should pray that the Word of God will be preached with great power (1 Cor. 2:4); that God Himself will speak to us and to each person in the congregation through the act of preaching. We should pray that God would send visitors in whose hearts He is at work. We should also pray that God would use the worship service and the sermon to call many to faith in Christ (Rom. 10:14, 15; 1 Cor. 14:24, 25). In addition to a time of private prayer, pray together as a family before you leave for church, asking God to meet with you and the congregation.

Furthermore, we need to pray for the Spirit's help in worship: that He will manifest God's presence to us; that He will enable us to worship from the heart; that He will keep our minds from wandering. Pray as well for those leading worship that the Spirit will use them to lead us into the presence of God.

We may also prepare Saturday night or Sunday morning by prayerfully reflecting on the Scripture text on which the pastor will preach.[5] Pray about the meaning of the text and its application to you. If you have small children read the text to them, so they can begin to think about it. This exercise will enable us to profit much more from the preaching of the word.[6]

One other part of preparation is to have a plan for the day. As we have seen in the previous two chapters, we need to plan the day for ourselves and our children. Even if we do not have children, we will benefit by having goals for the day. What benefits are we seeking? What service can we give? What book do we want to read? We often forfeit the benefit of the day by approaching it in a haphazard manner and consequently doing little more than attending corporate worship.

Let me add, that although it is not directly a part of preparation, it is well to conclude the day with an inventory. Consider your use of the day and what you accomplished. Did you meet your goals? Thank the Lord for the day and ask Him to seal it to your well-being and to stir up in you a greater longing for the eternal Sabbath. Confess the sin that

---

5. If pastors are preaching through books of the Bible, it will be easy for the people to reflect ahead of time on the sermon text. If the pastor is not preaching a series, he could publicise his intended text the previous week.

6. *The Larger Catechism* 160 says that we should 'attend upon it (the preached word) with diligence, preparation, and prayer, ...'

marred the performance of all your duties and remind yourself that both you and your Sabbath-keeping are acceptable because of the perfect work of Christ. Consider what you can do differently in preparation for and in observance of the Sabbath.

The Sabbath is a beautiful park designed by God for your spiritual well-being. It is a day of spiritual re-creation; a 'market day of the soul'; a weekly holiday (holy-day) for God's people. Approach it as you would approach a special family outing or that special vacation so that you may discover the treasures of the day. Use it as God ordained for His honour and your well-being.

> Then you will take delight in the LORD,
> And I will make you ride on the heights of the earth;
> And I will feed you *with* the heritage of Jacob your father,
> For the mouth of the LORD has spoken (Isa. 58:14).

Appendix: Prayers For the Lord's Day

1. Taken from *Home Worship: A Series of Topical Prayers for Use in The Family Circle* by the late James W. Weir (Philadelphia: Presbyterian Board of Publication), pp.216, 220, 223, 227, 230.

Sabbath Morning

Great God, thou hast commanded us, saying, 'Seek ye my face.' Thy face, Lord, we will seek, and oh, as thou art now pouring on the earth the refreshing light of morning, so do thou in our approach to thee lift upon us the light of thy countenance and shine into our hearts to give us the light of the knowledge of thy glory in the face of Jesus Christ, for it is in his merits we would seek acceptance and in his name we offer our petitions.

O Lord, we lift up again to thee our voice of thanksgiving for renewed mercy. We thank thee that thou hast not cut us off as cumberers of the ground, but hast given us another week of probation and hast brought us again under the gracious influence of the Sabbath. We bless thee, O God, for this day of rest from earthly toil, and of fellowship with thy people in solemn worship, and of meditation on our character and duties, and of communion with thee, the Father of spirits. We pray that no thoughts of worldly pleasure or honor or riches may intrude upon us this day. We pray that we may not be debarred from the privilege of meeting with thy people in the sanctuary, and while there may we sing thy praises, making melody in our hearts unto the Lord, in prayer lifting up in fervency and faith our desires unto thee, attending to thy word with diligence, preparation and prayer, receiving it with faith and love, laying it up in our hearts that we may practice it in our lives. We pray that those portions of this day which we may pass at home may be spent in the spirit of thy commandment, 'Remember the Sabbath-day to keep it holy.' Suffer us not in our household intercourse to break this statute by word or deed, but let there be a savor in our speech and actions in sacred harmony with this consecrated day. We pray that our minds may be directed to such themes of meditation and reading as will sanctify our spirits and quicken us in the Christian life. And we pray that we may enjoy a spirit of supplication before thee this day, with reverence and confidence and importunity seeking thy blessing on ourselves and on thy Church and on a perishing world.

Lord, bless those who shall minister in holy things this day. Give them the unction of the Holy One. Let the love of God and of truth and of souls animate them in all the duties of the sanctuary. Give them wisdom to understand and zeal to declare the whole counsel of God. Oh, may they, as they stand between the living and the dead, encourage thy people in the narrow way of righteousness and salvation and warn the ungodly to flee from the broad way of sin and death. Oh, give them a precious reward for their labor in beholding they people quickened according to thy word, in being instruments of converting sinners unto thee, in the enjoyment of gospel-blessings in their own souls, and in the reward of those that shine as the brightness of the firmament and as the stars for ever.

O Lord, bless thy people this day. Let the worship they shall offer thee be full of faith and fervency, and be answered by blessings on themselves and others. Let the truth they hear instruct and quicken and sanctify them, that they may cry out, 'How amiable are thy tabernacles, O Lord of hosts! A day in thy courts is better than a thousand. We had rather be doorkeepers in thy house than to dwell in the tents of wickedness.' Make their necessary household and social intercourse this day consistent with holy time and mutually profitable for Sabbath-day blessings. Let thy testimonies and works and ways be their meditation. And, O Thou that seest in secret, but rewardest openly, may they enter into their closet and enjoy to-day precious seasons of communion with thee, the Father of spirits.

And now, Lord, we pray that thy precept, 'Remember the Sabbath-day to keep it holy,' may have unwonted power over the consciences and conduct of the impenitent. Oh, let an increased number of the careless and ungodly be gathered at this time into thy sanctuaries. May they join in every service with respect and seriousness and listen to the preached word with attention and conviction. Oh, let the truth be seasonable to every mind, and be to many a savor of life unto life. Gracious God, send thy Spirit into every assembly, that the careless may be alarmed and the impenitent convicted and the stubborn subdued, so that in every temple of God souls may be converted to thee and this be a day of the right hand of the Most High. Amen.

Sabbath Morning

Gracious God, we thank thee for the mercies of the last week, that thou hast nurtured and protected us, so that we behold the light of another Sabbath in peace and comfort. We come now to thee in the name of our Mediator and Advocate for that frame of spirit which becomes this sacred season, and for those blessings which the proper use of these consecrated hours will secure to us.

We beseech thee to enable us to remember the Sabbath-day to keep it holy. In six days thou didst make heaven, earth and sea, and didst rest the seventh day; wherefore thou hast blessed the Sabbath and hallowed it. We thank thee, God of mercy, for this consecrated season, in which thou givest rest to our wearied natures and affordest us leisure for reflection on our duties in this world and our destinies in the world to come. We thank thee for its privileges of praise and of prayer and of instruction, by which thy saints are built up in faith and zeal and sinners are brought from the darkness and iniquity of carnal nature to the light and holiness of heavenly grace. We would praise thee that there still remaineth this rest for the people of God. Thou hast made the Sabbath for man, and thou hast abolished neither its privileges nor duties, but wilt continue them down to the end of the world.

Oh that we might always be in the spirit on the Lord's day. May we remember that thou hast given us six days of the week for our own employments and hast challenged a special ownership of the seventh, and that thou hast given it the sanction of thine own example and blessing. Oh, let us not profane that holy time by idleness, nor by doing that which in itself is sinful, nor by unnecessary thoughts, words or works about worldly employments or recreations. May we sanctify it by a holy resting, even from such avocations as are lawful on other days, and spend all its sacred hours in the public and private exercises of thy worship, except so much as must be taken up in the works of necessity and mercy. Oh, let this day ever be a precious occasion, wherein thy love shall be richly manifested to us and our affections hold free and holy and rejoicing communion with thy Spirit. May we be prepared by its sanctifying duties and reviving pleasures for serving thee and mankind better in all the relations of life. Oh, make it a blessed type of that eternal Sabbath which is reserved for the pure in heart in the regions of unmingled bliss.

Lord of the Sabbath, save this holy day from the desecration which has been so fearfully brought upon it. Thou seest how men pursue on it their carnal pleasures and worldly interests regardless of thy statutes and the ultimate welfare of their country and of mankind. Even those who have made a covenant with thee by sacrifice sometimes join hand in hand with the ungodly in these profanations of sacred time. Oh that thy people would set their faces as flint against these transgressions and bear the testimony of their voice and conduct against them. Bring not thy wrath upon our land because its inhabitants make the Sabbath their season of amusement, convenience and gain. Oh, teach all men that it is thy will that they sanctify that day, and that thou hast judgments in store for its transgressors; whilst they who turn away their feet from polluting it and from doing their pleasure upon it, and who shall call the Sabbath a delight, the holy of the Lord, honorable, shall be fed with the heritage of Jacob, for the mouth of the Lord hath spoken it.

Lord, bless, we pray thee, in the name of Jesus, thy preached word this day. Give wisdom, grace and fervor to those who shall be called to preach the words of life. Let not thy word be as the seed which fell by the wayside, nor as that which fell on stony ground, nor as that which fell among thorns, but as that which fell upon good ground. Oh, do thou seal instruction upon every heart. Teach the ignorant, arouse the careless, alarm the stupid, turn the gainsaying, melt the hardened, sanctify the unholy, encourage the timid, strengthen the zealous, and let grace, mercy and peace rest upon every worshiping assembly.

O Lord, we humbly pray in Christ's name for the remission of all our sins, and for a new and sanctified consecration of ourselves to thee for time and eternity. Amen.

Sabbath Morning

Lord of the Sabbath, we thank thee for another of the days of the Son of man. Oh, let it be like the sun which brings it, a messenger of light and joy to the world. We thank thee for its abundant blessings to us in times past, and we supplicate thee that its return to-day may bring us new and increasing benefits. But we have come to thee this morning in the name of Jesus to plead specially for thy blessing on thy word as it shall be preached to those to whom the Sabbath has never yet come with sanctifying and saving power.

O Lord, let the ministrations of thy house this day instruct the ignorant. Oh, gather into thy courts many who have kept away from instruction until their foolish hearts are darkened, and who live in a land of gospel light in almost heathenish ignorance of religious truth and duty. Oh that they might incline their ears to wisdom and apply their hearts to understanding. And, Lord, we pray that thou wouldst instruct by thy truth this day those who sit from Sabbath to Sabbath under the gospel with ears that hear not and hearts that perceive not the truth. Oh, dispel their listlessness and vagrancy of mind, and let scores and hundreds of unthinking hearers be made wise unto salvation.

Let the ministrations of thy house this day arrest the careless and bring them to an anxious inquiry what they must do to be saved. How long, O Lord, shall the corrupting cares of earth absorb the solicitude of beings whom thou hast made in the image of thine eternity, who are living in a state of trial for an endless life, on whom condemnation for sin even now rests, whose days on earth are a shadow, and who, if death finds them unconverted, must dwell with everlasting burnings? O God, startle the deep anxieties of their souls. Make them cry out in anguish of spirit, "Men and brethren, what shall we do?" And make the way of truth so plain, so clear, to them that by thy grace they may believe on the Lord Jesus Christ and be saved.

O Lord, alarm this day stupid sinners whose consciences are seared as with a hot iron. Lo! the creatures whom thou hast made to know thy name and love thy character and enjoy thy bounty and do thy will live almost as heedless of thee as the brutes that perish. Lord, awake such speedily from their guilty and degrading and ruinous stupor. Arouse them by thy Spirit to a sense of their sin and misery and danger, and give them newness of life through the Lord Jesus Christ.

O Lord, convince the gainsaying. Oh that those who doubt or deny or oppose the truth as it is in Jesus might have every thought of their hearts brought into captivity to the obedience of Christ. Thou hast magnified thy mercy in sparing these scoffers and blasphemers. Thou hast glorified the truth in those defenses of religion which have restrained the influences of infidelity. Lord, magnify thy name, and with increasing glory, by turning this unbelief to faith and this scorn to praise and this hatred to love.

Subdue the hardened. Let thy word this day be as a fire that melteth and as a hammer that breaketh rock. Oh, there is not heart so stony but thou canst turn it into a heart of flesh; there is not will so stubborn but thou canst make it pliant. To thee they are all as clay in the hands of the potter.

Gracious God, make them examples of tender-hearted submission to thy will.

Sanctify the unholy. Let the great commission of thy Spirit to convince men of sin be consummated in all thy sanctuaries this day. Let penitence work in every heart. May the grace that bringeth salvation teach men to deny ungodliness. Make them clean through the word that shall be spoken to them. Sanctify them by thy truth: thy word is truth.

O Lord, encourage the timid. If there be any who halt between two opinions and tremble to choose the Lord lest he should not choose them, assure them that whosoever cometh unto thee thou wilt in no wise cast out. If there be any who have made a covenant with thee by sacrifice, but whose hope of acceptance is disturbed by fears, enable them this day to know Him whom they have believed.

Strengthen the zealous. Refresh and increase their knowledge of truth and duty. Give them new motives to obedience and new purposes of well-doing. While they strive to work out their own salvation, make them zealous of good works toward a perishing world and instruments for its redemption from woe to bliss.

O Lord, we humbly and earnestly pray in the name of Jesus that thy preached word may have free course everywhere and be glorified. May it benefit our souls in all our spiritual wants. And the praise of all shall be thine for ever. Amen.

Sabbath Evening

Our Father in heaven, we have come to thee this night to thank thee for the privileges of this day. Oh, let the meditations of our hearts and the words of our mouths be acceptable to thee through Jesus Christ our Redeemer, who is Lord of the Sabbath.

Gracious God, we acknowledge thy distinguishing mercy in making us partakers of Sabbath-day blessings. Though this day has come with the light of the sun upon all the tribes of earth, yet it has brought no dayspring from on high of spiritual blessings to many, very many, nations of the world. For, lo! in thine inscrutable wisdom they dwell in the shadow of death. Thou hast not withheld from them any right or done them any injustice, and in that day when thou wilt justify thy ways to men we all shall see and own that justice as well as judgment is the habitation of thy throne. But any privileges above them which we are permitted to enjoy we humbly and thankfully acknowledge to be the fruits of free, sovereign, distinguishing, unmerited grace.

Give us now an abiding conviction that these repeated and increasing mercies demand repeated and increasing exercises of thanksgiving and acts of obedience. Thou hast taught us that thou wilt require much of him to whom thou hast given much, and that he who knows his master's will, but does it not, shall be beaten with many stripes. Oh, let not this condemnation rest upon us; let not these Sabbaths be so neglected or abused as to prove witnesses against us, either in thy dispensations of justice on the earth or in thy retributions in the world to come. But may we use them so diligently that we shall continually grow in grace and in meetness for the heavenly Sabbath that rest which remaineth for the people of God.

O Lord, let thy blessing rest upon the services of this Sabbath. Hear and answer the supplications which have this day gone up from the closet sacrifice and from the family altar and from the temple-offering. Wherever thy word has been read in retirement or among the household let it be a savor of knowledge and life. Let thy life-giving favor abide upon those whose meditations have been heavenward. But chiefly we desire that thy blessing may rest with unwonted power upon thy preached word. Make it an effectual means of convincing and converting sinners and building them up in holiness and comfort through faith unto salvation. Thou hast indeed put this treasure in earthen vessels that the excellency might be of God. We seek not the glory of any human instruments, but do thou honor thy power in using them as means for human salvation. Oh, let not the truths which have been spoken be lost in the air like the sounds which uttered them, but let them be so commended by thy Spirit to those who heard them that they shall be impressed on their reason and memory and will and conscience and affection, convincing the impenitent of the enormous guilt of their transgression, showing them the fearful danger of their rebellion, inclining them to deep repentance for their wickedness, displaying to them the countless riches of salvation in Jesus, and persuading them to a saving faith in his precious atonement. Lord, let this Sabbath be signalized in the history of man's redemption by manifold displays of converting grace.

O Lord, we humbly invoke thy blessing in behalf of those who profess thy name. Let thy word be a discerner of the thoughts of their hearts. If any have been deceived by a name to live, reveal to them their true character and give them repentance and remission and a new and sanctified and unreserved consecration of themselves to Christ, and let none such be suffered to draw back to perdition, but be enabled to believe unto the saving of their souls.

O Lord, let rich and rejoicing and everlasting blessings

follow thy truth in the hearts of all who belong to the commonwealth of Israel and the covenant of promise. Let it increase their knowledge and strengthen their faith and elevate their hope and inflame their love and quicken their zeal. Let this Sabbath send its influence upon their character and conduct through the coming week, and onward through life and upward through eternity.

Forgive wherein we have thought or said or done amiss this day. Pardon the sins of our holy services. Blot out all our transgressions of every kind and degree. Make us clean through the word thou hast spoken unto us. Sanctify us by thy truth: thy word is truth. And thine, Father, Son and Spirit shall be the praise. Amen.

Sabbath Evening

O Lord, the eyes of all are unto thee, and thou givest them their meat in due season; thou openest thy hand and satisfiest the desires of every living thing. But if thy care and compassion are thus exercised toward our temporal wants, may we not hope that when our desires for spiritual favors are directed to thee thou wilt satisfy them? Nay, thou hast told us that if we seek thy kingdom and righteousness all these things shall be added to us. Give us, therefore, in the name of Jesus, a gracious acceptance while we seek thy blessing upon this Sabbath.

We mourn before thee, O God, that there are any around us (and, alas! how many there are!) who have forgotten to remember this Sabbath day to keep it holy, and who, whilst thou hast been giving them its sacred hours that they might learn repentance and faith and salvation, have sought their own pleasure and dishonored this day and offended God. Lord, arouse them by a conviction of their folly and guilt, incline them to forsake their profanations, and lead them to a consecration of this blessed season to thy service. And we ask this result not only for those around us, but for Sabbath-breakers everywhere. Wherever this iniquity has been framed by law let it be blotted from the statute-book, and let this people and every other so act in their national and individual relations as to receive the promised blessing of those who keep thy Sabbath from polluting it.

We thank thee, O Lord, for the multitudes who have been gathered this day into thy courts for thy worship. Though this earth is a degenerate, apostate, rebellious world, yet in these precious Sabbaths we behold the hope of its recovery to God. We thank thee for those ministrations in which we have shared this day. Forgive wherein we have been thoughtless or irreverent. Remember those praises which we sung to thy name. Oh, give us an increasing impression of thine excellence, so that these ascriptions of honor may be the honest expressions of our hearts. Remember the prayers we offer to thee in thy house. Answer them, we beseech thee, according to thy merciful wisdom and our real wants. Bless unto us thy preached word, and make it profitable to us for doctrine, for reproof, for correction and for instruction in righteousness.

Sanctify us unto all our domestic and private use of this day. If we have been led into thoughts or words or works inconsistent with it, forgive us and grant us purposes of new obedience in keeping it holy. Let the truths and duties on which we have conferred and read and meditated, and about which we have prayed, be treasured in our hearts and practiced in our lives.

Let gracious influences abide upon all who this day have sat under the droppings of thy sanctuary. Oh, let not its words of praise and prayer and instruction be as sounds that die in the air, or as water that is spilled on the ground and cannot be gathered. Let them not be swift witnesses against any for neglect or perversion or gainsaying. Make them in every congregation a savor of life unto life, rejoicing and quickening the hearts of thy people, convincing and converting sinners, and adding to thy Church many of such as shall be saved.

O Lord, we ask thy blessing upon the instruction given this day in Sunday-schools. Let every faithful teacher carry in his own bosom a reward for his labor of love, and come back to it with renewed and enlarged zeal and knowledge and prayerfulness. If any have been unfaithful in their work, show them their delinquency, give them repentance for it, and bring them again to their duty resolved in thy strength to seek the blessing of those whom, being faithful over a few things, thou wilt make rulers over many things. Lord, seal instruction upon the youthful mind. May they acknowledge thy claims upon their hearts, and now, while they are in the dew of their youth, and before the evil days come, may they remember their Creator and serve thee in newness of life.

Gracious God, we beseech thee to grant us they favor in all the things thou seest we need. If we ask amiss, forgive; if we fail to ask, bestow; and let our persons and services be accepted before thee in Jesus our Redeemer. Amen.

2. From *The Valley of Vision* (A Collection of Puritan Prayers & Devotions), edited by Arthur Bennett (The Banner of Truth Trust, 1975), pp. 195, 199, 209, 210.

Lord's Day Morning

O MAKER AND UPHOLDER OF ALL THINGS,
> Day and night are thine; they are also mine from thee –
>> the night to rid me of the cares of the day,
>>> to refresh my weary body,
>>> to renew my natural strength;
>> the day to summon me to new activities,
>>> to give me opportunity to glorify thee,
>>> to serve my generation,
>>> to acquire knowledge, holiness, eternal life.
> But one day above all days is made especially
>> for thy honour and my improvement;
> The sabbath reminds me of thy rest from creation,
>> of the resurrection of my Saviour,
>> of his entering into repose,
> Thy house is mine,
>> but I am unworthy to met thee there,
>> and am unfit for spiritual service.
> When I enter it I come before thee as a sinner,
>> condemned by conscience and thy Word,
> For I am still in the body and in the wilderness,
>> ignorant, weak, in danger,
>> and in need of thine aid.
> But encouraged by thy all-sufficient grace
>> let me go to thy house with a lively hope of
>>> meeting thee,
>> knowing that there thou wilt come to me and give
>>> me peace.
> My soul is drawn out to thee in longing desires
>> for thy presence in the sanctuary, at the table,
>> where all are entertained on a feast of good things;
> Let me before the broken elements, emblems of thy dying love,
>> cry to thee with broken heart for grace and forgiveness.
> I long for that blissful communion of thy people
>> in thy eternal house in the perfect kingdom;
> These are they that follow the Lamb;
> May I be of their company!

Lord's Day evening

MOST HOLY GOD,
May the close of an earthly sabbath
         remind me that the last of them will one day end.
Animate me with joy that in heaven praise will never cease,
         that adoration will continue for ever,
         that no flesh will grow weary,
                  no congregations disperse,
                  no affections flag,
                  no thoughts wander,
                  no will droop,
                  but all will be adoring love.
Guard my mind from making ordinances my stay or trust,
                           from hewing out broken cisterns,
                           from resting on outward helps.
Wing me through earthly forms to thy immediate presence;
May my feeble prayers show me the emptiness and vanity of my sins;
Deepen in me the conviction that my most fervent prayers,
         and most lowly confessions, need to be repented of.
May my best services bring me nearer to the cross,
         and prompt me to cry, 'None but Jesus!'
By thy Spirit give abiding life to the lessons of this day:
May the seed sown take deep root and yield a full harvest.
Let all who see me take knowledge that I have been with thee
         that thou hast taught me my need as a sinner,
                  hast revealed a finished salvation to me,
                  hast enriched me with all spiritual blessings,
                  hast chosen me to show forth Jesus to others,
                  hast helped me to dispel the mists of unbelief.
O great creator, mighty protector, gracious preserver,
                  thou dost load me with lovingkindnesses,
                  and hast made me thy purchased possession,
                  and redeemed me from all guilt;
I praise and bless thee for my sabbath rest, my calm conscience,
                                              my peace of heart.

First Day Morning Worship

O LORD,
We commune with thee every day,
    but week days are worldly days,
    and secular concerns reduce heavenly impressions.
We bless thee therefore for the day sacred to our souls
    when we can wait upon thee and be refreshed;
We thank thee for the institutions of religion
    by use of which we draw near to thee and thou to us;
We rejoice in another Lord's Day
    when we call off our minds from the cares of the world
    and attend upon thee without distraction;
Let our retirement be devout,
    our conversation edifying,
    our reading pious,
    our hearing profitable,
        that our souls may be quickened and elevated.
We are going to the house of prayer,
    pour upon us the spirit of grace and supplication;
We are going to the house of praise,
    awaken in us every grateful and cheerful emotion;
We are going to the house of instruction,
    give testimony to the Word preached,
    and glorify it in the hearts of all who hear;
    may it enlighten the ignorant,
        awaken the careless, reclaim the wandering,
        establish the weak, comfort the feeble-minded,
        make ready a people for their Lord.
Be a sanctuary to all who cannot come,
Forget not those who never come,
And do thou bestow upon us
        benevolence towards our dependents,
        forgiveness towards our enemies,
        peaceableness towards our neighbours,
        openness towards our fellow-Christians.

First Day Evening

The Teacher

O GOD,
We bless thee
    our creator, preserver, benefactor, teacher,
        for opening to us the volume of nature
        where we may read and consider thy works.
Thou hast this day spread before us the fuller pages of revelation,
        and in them we see what thou wouldest have us do,
           what thou requirest of us,
           what thou hast done for us,
           what thou hast promised to us,
           what thou hast given us in Jesus.
We pray thee for a conscious experience of his salvation,
        in our deliverance from sin,
        in our bearing his image,
        in our enjoying his presence,
        in our being upheld by his free Spirit.
Let us not live uncertain of what we are,
        of where we are going.
Bear witness with our spirit that we are thy children;
And enable each one to say, 'I know my redeemer.'
Bless us with a growing sense of this salvation.
If already enlightened in Christ, may we see greater things;
If quickened, may we have more abundant life;
If renewed, let us go on from strength to strength.
Give us closer abiding in Jesus that we may
        bring forth more fruit,
        have a deeper sense of our obligations to him,
           that we may surrender all,
        have a fuller joy,
           that we may serve him more completely.
And may our faith work by love
        towards him who died,
        towards our fellow-believers,
        towards our fellow-men.

3. *The Practice of Piety A Puritan Devotional Manual* by Lewis Bayly, D.D., (Morgan, PA: Soli Deo Gloria Publications, [London: Hamilton, Adams, and Co., 1842]), pp. 193, 203.

A Morning Prayer for the Sabbath-day.

O Lord most high, O God eternal, all whose works are glorious, and whose thoughts are very deep: there can be no better thing, than to praise thy name, and to declare thy loving-kindness in the morning, on thy holy and blessed Sabbath day! For it is thy will and commandment, that we should sanctify this day in thy service and praise: and in the thankful remembrance, as of the creation of the world by the power of thy word; so of the redemption of mankind by the death of thy Son. Thine, O Lord, I confess, is greatness and power, and glory and victory, and praise; for all that is in heaven and earth is thine: thine is the kingdom, O Lord, and thou excellest as head over all. Both riches and honour come of thee, and thou reignest over all, and in thine hand is power and strength; and in thine hand it is to make great, and to give grace unto all. Now, therefore, O my God, I praise thy glorious name, that whereas I, a wretched sinner, having so many ways provoked thy majesty to anger and displeasure; thou notwithstanding, of thy favour and goodness, passing by my profaneness and infirmities, hast vouchsafed to add this Sabbath again to the number of my days. And vouchsafe, O heavenly Father, for the merits of Jesus Christ thy Son, whose glorious resurrection thy whole church celebrateth this day, to pardon and forgive me all my sins and misdeeds. Especially, O Lord [Here thou mayest confess whatsoever sin of the last week clogs thy conscience] cleanse my soul from those filthy sins, with the blood of thy most pure and undefiled Lamb, which taketh away the sins of the world. And let thy Holy Spirit more and more subdue my corruptions, that I may be renewed after thy own image, to serve thee in newness of life, and holiness of conversation. And as of thy mercy thou hast brought me to the beginning of this blessed day; so I beseech thee make it a day of reconciliation between my sinful soul and thy divine majesty. Give me grace to make it a day of repentance unto thee, that thy goodness may seal it to be a day of pardon unto me; and that I may remember that the keeping holy of this day is a commandment which thy own finger hath written; that on this day I might meditate on the glorious works of our creation and redemption, and learn how to know and keep all the rest of thy holy laws and commandments. And when anon, I shall, with the rest of the holy assembly, appear before thy presence in thy house, to offer unto thee our morning sacrifice of praise and prayer, and to hear what thy Spirit, by the preaching of thy word, and to hear what thy Spirit, by the preaching of thy word, shall speak unto thy servant, O let not my sins stand as a cloud to stop my prayers from ascending unto thee, or to keep back thy grace from descending by thy word into my heart. I know, O Lord, and tremble to think, that three parts of the good seed falls upon bad ground. O let not my heart be like the highway, which through hardness, and want of true understanding, receives not the seed, till the evil one cometh and catcheth it away: nor like to the stony ground, which heareth with joy for a time, but falleth away as soon as persecution ariseth for the Gospel's sake: nor like the thorny ground, which by the cares of this world, and the deceitfulness of riches, choketh the word which it heareth, and makes it altogether unfruitful; but that like unto the good ground, I may hear thy word, with an honest and good heart understand it, and keep it, and bring forth fruit with patience, in that measure that thy wisdom shall think meet for thy glory, and mine everlasting comfort. Open likewise, I beseech thee, O Lord, the door of utterance unto thy faithful servant, whom thou hast sent unto us to open our eyes, that we may turn from darkness to light, and from the power of Satan unto God: that we may receive forgiveness of sins, and inheritance among them which are sanctified by faith in Christ. And give me grace to submit myself unto his ministry, as well when he terrifieth me with judgments, as when he comforteth me with thy mercies; and that I may have him in singular love for his works' sake; because he watcheth for my soul as he that must give an account for the same unto his master. And give me grace to behave myself in the holy congregation with comeliness and reverence, as in thy presence, and in the sight of thy holy angels: keep me from drowsiness and sleeping, and from all wandering thoughts, and worldly imaginations. Sanctify my memory, that it may be apt to receive, and firm to remember, those good and profitable doctrines which shall be taught unto us out of thy word. And that through the assistance of thy Holy Spirit, I may put the same lessons in practice for my direction in prosperity, for my consolation in misery, for the amendment of my life, and the glory of thy name. And that this day which godless and profane persons spend in their own lusts and pleasures, I, as one of thy obedient servants, may make my chief delight to consecrate to thy glory and honour, not doing mine own ways, nor seeking mine own will, nor speaking a vain word; but that, ceasing from the works of sin as well as from the works of my ordinary calling, I may, through thy blessing, feel in my heart the

beginning of that eternal Sabbath, which in unspeakable joy
and glory I shall celebrate with saints and angels, to thy
praise and worship, in thy heavenly kingdom for evermore.
All which I humbly crave at thy hands, in the name and
mediation of my Lord Jesus, in that form of prayer which he
hath taught me: "Our Father which art in heaven, hallowed
be thy name," &c.

A private Evening Prayer for the Lord's day.

O holy, holy, holy Lord God of Sabaoth! Suffer me, who am
but dust and ashes, to speak unto thy most glorious majesty.
I know that thou art a consuming fire; I acknowledge that I
am but withered stubble: my sins are in thy sight, and Satan
stands at my right hand to accuse me for them. I come not
to excuse but to judge myself worthy of all those judgments
which thy justice might most justly inflict upon me, a
wretched creature, for my sins and transgressions. The
number of them is so great, the nature of them is so grievous,
that they make me seem vile in my own eyes; how much
more loathsome in they sight? I confess they make me so far
from being worthy to be called thy son, that I am altogether
unworthy to have the name of thy meanest servant; and if
thou shouldst but recompense me according to my desert,
the earth, as weary of such a sinful burden, should open her
mouth and swallow me up, like one of Dathan's family, into
the bottomless pit of hell. For if thou didst not spare the
natural branches, those angels of glorious excellency, but
didst hurl them down from the heavenly habitations into the
pains of hellish darkness, to be kept unto damnation, when
they sinned but once against thy Majesty, and didst expel
our first parents out of paradise when they did but transgress
one of thy laws; alas! what vengeance may I expect, who

have not offended in one sin only, heaping daily sin upon sin without any true repentance, drinking iniquity as it were water, ever pouring in but never pouring out any filthiness, and have transgressed not one, but all thy holy laws and commandments? Yea, this present day which thou hast straitly commanded me to keep holy to thy praise and worship, I have not so religiously kept and observed, nor prepared my soul in that holiness and purity of heart, as was fit to meet thy blessed Majesty in the holy assembly of the saints. I have not attended to the preaching of thy word, nor to the administration of thy sacraments, with that humility, reverence, and devotion that I should: for though I was present at those holy exercises in my body, yet, Lord, I was overtaken with much drowsiness; and when I was awake my mind was so distracted and carried away with vain and worldly thoughts, that my soul seemed to be absent and out of the church. I have not so duly, as I should, meditated with myself, not conferred with my family upon those good instructions which we have heard and received out of thy holy word by the public ministry: for default of which, Satan hath stolen the most part of those instructions out of my heart, and I, wretched creature, have forgotten them as though they had never been heard. And my family doth not thrive in knowledge and sanctification under my government, as they should. Though I know where many of my poor brethren live in want and necessity, and some in pain, and comfortless; yet I have not remembered to relieve the one with my alms, nor the other with consolations; but I have feasted myself and satisfied my own lusts. I have spent the most part of the day in idle talk and vain exercises; yea, Lord, I have, &c. [Here confess whatsoever fault thou hast done that day by omission or commission, and then fetching from thy heart a deep sigh, say] and for all these my sins, my conscience cries guilty, thy law condemns me, and I am in thy hand to receive the sentence and the curse due to the wilful breach of so holy a commandment. But what if I am by thy law condemned? yet, Lord, thy gospel assures me that thy mercy is above all thy works; that thy grace transcends thy law; and thy goodness delighteth there to reign where sins do most abound. In the multitude of thy mercies, and for the merits of Jesus Christ my Saviour, I beseech thee, O Lord, who despisest not the sighings of a contrite heart, nor desirest the death of a penitent sinner, to pardon and forgive me all those my sins, and all the errors of this day and of my whole life, and free my soul from that curse and judgment which is due unto me for them. Thou that didst justify the contrite publican for four words of confession, and receive the prodigal child, when he had spent all the stock of thy grace, into favour upon his repentance; pardon my sins likewise, O Lord, and suffer me not to perish for my transgressions. O spare me, and receive me into thy favour again. Wilt thou, O Lord, who hast received all publicans, harlots, and sinners, that upon repentance sued to thee for grace, reject me? shall I alone be excluded from thy mercy? Far be it from me to think so: for thou art the same God of mercy to me that thou wast to them, and thy compassions never fail. Wherefore, O Lord, deal not with me after my merits, but according to thy great mercy; execute not thy severe justice against me a sinner, but exercise thy long-sufferance in forbearing thy own creature. I have nothing to present unto thee for a satisfaction, but only those bloody wounds, bitter death and passion, which thy blessed Son, my only Saviour, hath suffered for me. Him, in whom only thou art well pleased,

I offer unto thee for all my sins wherewith thou art displeased: him, my Mediator, the request of whose blood, speaking better things than that of Abel, thy mercy can never gainsay. Illuminate my understanding and sanctify my heart with thy Holy Spirit, that it may bring to my remembrance all those good and profitable lessons which this day and at other times have been taught me out of thy holy word; that I may remember thy commandments to keep them thy judgments to avoid them and thy sweet promises to rely upon them, in time of misery and distress. And now, O Lord, I resign myself to thy most holy will: O receive me into thy favour, and so draw me by thy grace unto thyself, that I may as well be thine by love and imitation as by calling and creation. And give me grace so to keep holy thy Sabbaths in this life, that when this life is ended, I may, with all thy saints and angels, celebrate an eternal Sabbath of joy and praise to the honour of thy most glorious name, in thy heavenly kingdom for evermore. Amen.

4. *Home Worship: A Series of Topical Prayers for Use in The Family Circle*, by the late James W. Weir (Philadelphia: Presbyterian Board of Publication), pp. 216, 220, 223, 227, 230.

Sabbath Morning

Great God, thou hast commanded us, saying, 'Seek ye my face.' Thy face, Lord, we will seek, and oh, as thou art now pouring on the earth the refreshing light of morning, so do thou in our approach to thee lift upon us the light of thy countenance and shine into our hearts to give us the light of the knowledge of thy glory in the face of Jesus Christ, for it is in his merits we would seek acceptance and in his name we offer our petitions.

O Lord, we lift up again to thee our voice of thanksgiving for renewed mercy. We thank thee that thou hast not cut us off as cumberers of the ground, but hast given us another week of probation and hast brought us again under the gracious influence of the Sabbath. We bless thee, O God, for this day of rest from earthly toil, and of fellowship with thy people in solemn worship, and of meditation on our character and duties, and of communion with thee, the Father of spirits. We pray that no thoughts of worldly pleasure or honor or riches may intrude upon us this day. We pray that we may not be debarred from the privilege of meeting with thy people in the sanctuary, and while there may we sing thy praises, making melody in our hearts unto the Lord, in prayer lifting up in fervency and faith our desires unto thee, attending to thy word with diligence, preparation and prayer, receiving it with faith and love, laying it up in our hearts that we may practice it in our lives. We pray that those portions of this day which we may pass at home may be spent in the spirit of thy commandment, 'Remember the Sabbath-day to keep it holy.' Suffer us not in our household intercourse to break this statute by word or deed, but let there be a savor in our speech and actions in sacred harmony with this consecrated day. We pray that our minds may be directed to such themes of meditation and reading as will sanctify our spirits and quicken us in the Christian life. And we pray that we may enjoy a spirit of supplication before thee this day, with reverence and confidence and importunity seeking thy blessing on ourselves and on thy Church and on a perishing world.

Lord, bless those who shall minister in holy things this day. Give them the unction of the Holy One. Let the love of

God and of truth and of souls animate them in all the duties of the sanctuary. Give them wisdom to understand and zeal to declare the whole counsel of God. Oh, may they, as they stand between the living and the dead, encourage thy people in the narrow way of righteousness and salvation and warn the ungodly to flee from the broad way of sin and death. Oh, give them a precious reward for their labor in beholding they people quickened according to thy word, in being instruments of converting sinners unto thee, in the enjoyment of gospel-blessings in their own souls, and in the reward of those that shine as the brightness of the firmament and as the stars for ever.

O Lord, bless thy people this day. Let the worship they shall offer thee be full of faith and fervency, and be answered by blessings on themselves and others. Let the truth they hear instruct and quicken and sanctify them, that they may cry out, 'How amiable are thy tabernacles, O Lord of hosts! A day in thy courts is better than a thousand. We had rather be doorkeepers in thy house than to dwell in the tents of wickedness.' Make their necessary household and social intercourse this day consistent with holy time and mutually profitable for Sabbath-day blessings. Let thy testimonies and works and ways be their meditation. And, O Thou that seest in secret, but rewardest openly, may they enter into their closet and enjoy to-day precious seasons of communion with thee, the Father of spirits.

And now, Lord, we pray that thy precept, 'Remember the Sabbath-day to keep it holy,' may have unwonted power over the consciences and conduct of the impenitent. Oh, let an increased number of the careless and ungodly be gathered at this time into thy sanctuaries. May they join in every service with respect and seriousness and listen to the preached word with attention and conviction. Oh, let the truth be seasonable to every mind, and be to many a savor of life unto life. Gracious God, send thy Spirit into every assembly, that the careless may be alarmed and the impenitent convicted and the stubborn subdued, so that in every temple of God souls may be converted to thee and this be a day of the right hand of the Most High. Amen.

Sabbath Morning

Gracious God, we thank thee for the mercies of the last week, that thou hast nurtured and protected us, so that we behold the light of another Sabbath in peace and comfort. We come now to thee in the name of our Mediator and Advocate for that frame of spirit which becomes this sacred season, and for those blessings which the proper use of these consecrated hours will secure to us.

We beseech thee to enable us to remember the Sabbath-day to keep it holy. In six days thou didst make heaven, earth and sea, and didst rest the seventh day; wherefore thou hast blessed the Sabbath and hallowed it. We thank thee, God of mercy, for this consecrated season, in which thou givest rest to our wearied natures and affordest us leisure for reflection on our duties in this world and our destinies in the world to come. We thank thee for its privileges of praise and of prayer and of instruction, by which thy saints are built up in faith and zeal and sinners are brought from the darkness and iniquity of carnal nature to the light and holiness of heavenly grace. We would praise thee that there still remaineth this rest for the people of God. Thou hast made the Sabbath for man, and thou hast abolished neither its privileges nor duties, but wilt continue them down to the end of the world.

Oh that we might always be in the spirit on the Lord's

day. May we remember that thou hast given us six days of the week for our own employments and hast challenged a special ownership of the seventh, and that thou hast given it the sanction of thine own example and blessing. Oh, let us not profane that holy time by idleness, nor by doing that which in itself is sinful, nor by unnecessary thoughts, words or works about worldly employments or recreations. May we sanctify it by a holy resting, even from such avocations as are lawful on other days, and spend all its sacred hours in the public and private exercises of thy worship, except so much as must be taken up in the works of necessity and mercy. Oh, let this day ever be a precious occasion, wherein thy love shall be richly manifested to us and our affections hold free and holy and rejoicing communion with thy Spirit. May we be prepared by its sanctifying duties and reviving pleasures for serving thee and mankind better in all the relations of life. Oh, make it a blessed type of that eternal Sabbath which is reserved for the pure in heart in the regions of unmingled bliss.

Lord of the Sabbath, save this holy day from the desecration which has been so fearfully brought upon it. Thou seest how men pursue on it their carnal pleasures and worldly interests regardless of thy statutes and the ultimate welfare of their country and of mankind. Even those who have made a covenant with thee by sacrifice sometimes join hand in hand with the ungodly in these profanations of sacred time. Oh that thy people would set their faces as flint against these transgressions and bear the testimony of their voice and conduct against them. Bring not thy wrath upon our land because its inhabitants make the Sabbath their season of amusement, convenience and gain. Oh, teach all men that it is thy will that they sanctify that day, and that thou hast judgments in store for its transgressors; whilst they who turn away their feet from polluting it and from doing their pleasure upon it, and who shall call the Sabbath a delight, the holy of the Lord, honorable, shall be fed with the heritage of Jacob, for the mouth of the Lord hath spoken it.

Lord, bless, we pray thee, in the name of Jesus, thy preached word this day. Give wisdom, grace and fervor to those who shall be called to preach the words of life. Let not thy word be as the seed which fell by the wayside, nor as that which fell on stony ground, nor as that which fell among thorns, but as that which fell upon good ground. Oh, do thou seal instruction upon every heart. Teach the ignorant, arouse the careless, alarm the stupid, turn the gainsaying, melt the hardened, sanctify the unholy, encourage the timid, strengthen the zealous, and let grace, mercy and peace rest upon every worshiping assembly.

O Lord, we humbly pray in Christ's name for the remission of all our sins, and for a new and sanctified consecration of ourselves to thee for time and eternity. Amen.

Sabbath Morning

Lord of the Sabbath, we thank thee for another of the days of the Son of man. Oh, let it be like the sun which brings it, a messenger of light and joy to the world. We thank thee for its abundant blessings to us in times past, and we supplicate thee that its return to-day may bring us new and increasing benefits. But we have come to thee this morning in the name of Jesus to plead specially for thy blessing on thy word as it shall be preached to those to whom the Sabbath has never yet come with sanctifying and saving power.

O Lord, let the ministrations of thy house this day instruct the ignorant. Oh, gather into thy courts many who have kept away from instruction until their foolish hearts are darkened, and who live in a land of gospel light in almost heathenish ignorance of religious truth and duty. Oh that they might incline their ears to wisdom and apply their hearts to understanding. And, Lord, we pray that thou wouldst instruct by thy truth this day those who sit from Sabbath to Sabbath under the gospel with ears that hear not and hearts that perceive not the truth. Oh, dispel their listlessness and vagrancy of mind, and let scores and hundreds of unthinking hearers be made wise unto salvation.

Let the ministrations of thy house this day arrest the careless and bring them to an anxious inquiry what they must do to be saved. How long, O Lord, shall the corrupting cares of earth absorb the solicitude of beings whom thou hast made in the image of thine eternity, who are living in a state of trial for an endless life, on whom condemnation for sin even now rests, whose days on earth are a shadow, and who, if death finds them unconverted, must dwell with everlasting burnings? O God, startle the deep anxieties of their souls. Make them cry out in anguish of spirit, 'Men and brethren, what shall we do?' And make the way of truth so plain, so clear, to them that by thy grace they may believe on the Lord Jesus Christ and be saved.

O Lord, alarm this day stupid sinners whose consciences are seared as with a hot iron. Lo! the creatures whom thou hast made to know thy name and love thy character and enjoy thy bounty and do thy will live almost as heedless of thee as the brutes that perish. Lord, awake such speedily from their guilty and degrading and ruinous stupor. Arouse them by thy Spirit to a sense of their sin and misery and danger, and give them newness of life through the Lord Jesus Christ.

O Lord, convince the gainsaying. Oh that those who doubt or deny or oppose the truth as it is in Jesus might have every thought of their hearts brought into captivity to the obedience of Christ. Thou hast magnified thy mercy in sparing these scoffers and blasphemers. Thou hast glorified the truth in those defenses of religion which have restrained the influences of infidelity. Lord, magnify thy name, and with increasing glory, by turning this unbelief to faith and this scorn to praise and this hatred to love.

Subdue the hardened. Let thy word this day be as a fire that melteth and as a hammer that breaketh rock. Oh, there is not heart so stony but thou canst turn it into a heart of flesh; there is not will so stubborn but thou canst make it pliant. To thee they are all as clay in the hands of the potter. Gracious God, make them examples of tender-hearted submission to thy will.

Sanctify the unholy. Let the great commission of thy Spirit to convince men of sin be consummated in all thy sanctuaries this day. Let penitence work in every heart. May the grace that bringeth salvation teach men to deny ungodliness. Make them clean through the word that shall be spoken to them. Sanctify them by thy truth: thy word is truth.

O Lord, encourage the timid. If there be any who halt between two opinions and tremble to choose the Lord lest he should not choose them, assure them that whosoever cometh unto thee thou wilt in no wise cast out. If there be any who have made a covenant with thee by sacrifice, but whose hope of acceptance is disturbed by fears, enable them this day to know Him whom they have believed.

Strengthen the zealous. Refresh and increase their knowledge of truth and duty. Give them new motives to obedience and new purposes of well-doing. While they strive to work out their own salvation, make them zealous of good works toward a perishing world and instruments for its redemption from woe to bliss.

O Lord, we humbly and earnestly pray in the name of Jesus that thy preached word may have free course everywhere and be glorified. May it benefit our souls in all our spiritual wants. And the praise of all shall be thine for ever. Amen.

Sabbath Evening

Our Father in heaven, we have come to thee this night to thank thee for the privileges of this day. Oh, let the meditations of our hearts and the words of our mouths be acceptable to thee through Jesus Christ our Redeemer, who is Lord of the Sabbath.

Gracious God, we acknowledge thy distinguishing mercy in making us partakers of Sabbath-day blessings. Though this day has come with the light of the sun upon all the tribes of earth, yet it has brought no dayspring from on high of spiritual blessings to many, very many, nations of the world. For, lo! in thine inscrutable wisdom they dwell in the shadow of death. Thou hast not withheld from them any right or done them any injustice, and in that day when thou wilt justify thy ways to men we all shall see and own that justice as well as judgment is the habitation of thy throne. But any privileges above them which we are permitted to enjoy we humbly and thankfully acknowledge to be the fruits of free, sovereign, distinguishing, unmerited grace.

Give us now an abiding conviction that these repeated and increasing mercies demand repeated and increasing exercises of thanksgiving and acts of obedience. Thou hast taught us that thou wilt require much of him to whom thou hast given much, and that he who knows his master's will, but does it not, shall be beaten with many stripes. Oh, let not this condemnation rest upon us; let not these Sabbaths be so neglected or abused as to prove witnesses against us, either in thy dispensations of justice on the earth or in thy retributions in the world to come. But may we use them so diligently that we shall continually grow in grace and in meetness for the heavenly Sabbath that rest which remaineth for the people of God.

O Lord, let thy blessing rest upon the services of this Sabbath. Hear and answer the supplications which have this day gone up from the closet sacrifice and from the family altar and from the temple-offering. Wherever thy word has been read in retirement or among the household let it be a savor of knowledge and life. Let thy life-giving favor abide upon those whose meditations have been heavenward. But chiefly we desire that thy blessing may rest with unwonted power upon thy preached word. Make it an effectual means of convincing and converting sinners and building them up in holiness and comfort through faith unto salvation. Thou hast indeed put this treasure in earthen vessels that the excellency might be of God. We seek not the glory of any human instruments, but do thou honor thy power in using them as means for human salvation. Oh, let not the truths which have been spoken be lost in the air like the sounds which uttered them, but let them be so commended by thy Spirit to those who heard them that they shall be impressed on their reason and memory and will and conscience and affection, convincing the impenitent of the enormous guilt of their transgression, showing them the fearful danger of their rebellion, inclining them to deep repentance for their wickedness, displaying to them the countless riches of salvation in Jesus, and persuading them to a saving faith in his precious atonement. Lord, let this Sabbath be signalized in the history of man's redemption by manifold displays of converting grace.

O Lord, we humbly invoke thy blessing in behalf of those who profess thy name. Let thy word be a discerner of the thoughts of their hearts. If any have been deceived by a name to live, reveal to them their true character and give them repentance and remission and a new and sanctified and unreserved consecration of themselves to Christ, and let none such be suffered to draw back to perdition, but be enabled to believe unto the saving of their souls.

O Lord, let rich and rejoicing and everlasting blessings follow thy truth in the hearts of all who belong to the commonwealth of Israel and the covenant of promise. Let it increase their knowledge and strengthen their faith and elevate their hope and inflame their love and quicken their zeal. Let this Sabbath send its influence upon their character and conduct through the coming week, and onward through life and upward through eternity.

Forgive wherein we have thought or said or done amiss this day. Pardon the sins of our holy services. Blot out all our transgressions of every kind and degree. Make us clean through the word thou hast spoken unto us. Sanctify us by thy truth: thy word is truth. And thine, Father, Son and Spirit shall be the praise. Amen.

Sabbath Evening

O Lord, the eyes of all are unto thee, and thou givest them their meat in due season; thou openest thy hand and satisfiest the desires of every living thing. But if thy care and compassion are thus exercised toward our temporal wants, may we not hope that when our desires for spiritual favors are directed to thee thou wilt satisfy them? Nay, thou hast told us that if we seek thy kingdom and righteousness all these things shall be added to us. Give us, therefore, in the name of Jesus, a gracious acceptance while we seek thy blessing upon this Sabbath.

We mourn before thee, O God, that there are any around us (and, alas! how many there are!) who have forgotten to remember this Sabbath day to keep it holy, and who, whilst thou hast been giving them its sacred hours that they might learn repentance and faith and salvation, have sought their own pleasure and dishonored this day and offended God. Lord, arouse them by a conviction of their folly and guilt, incline them to forsake their profanations, and lead them to a consecration of this blessed season to thy service. And we ask this result not only for those around us, but for Sabbath-breakers everywhere. Wherever this iniquity has been framed by law let it be blotted from the statute-book, and let this people and every other so act in their national and individual relations as to receive the promised blessing of those who keep thy Sabbath from polluting it.

We thank thee, O Lord, for the multitudes who have been gathered this day into thy courts for thy worship. Though this earth is a degenerate, apostate, rebellious world, yet in these precious Sabbaths we behold the hope of its recovery to God. We thank thee for those ministrations in which we have shared this day. Forgive wherein we have been thoughtless or irreverent. Remember those praises which we sung to thy name. Oh, give us an increasing impression of thine excellence, so that these ascriptions of honor may be the honest expressions of our hearts. Remember the prayers we offer to thee in thy house. Answer them, we beseech thee, according to thy merciful wisdom and our real wants. Bless unto us thy preached word, and make it profitable to us for doctrine, for reproof, for correction and for instruction in righteousness.

Sanctify us unto all our domestic and private use of this day. If we have been led into thoughts or words or works inconsistent with it, forgive us and grant us purposes of new obedience in keeping it holy. Let the truths and duties on which we have conferred and read and meditated, and about which we have prayed, be treasured in our hearts and practiced in our lives.

Let gracious influences abide upon all who this day have sat under the droppings of thy sanctuary. Oh, let not its words of praise and prayer and instruction be as sounds that die in the air, or as water that is spilled on the ground and cannot be gathered. Let them not be swift witnesses against any for neglect or perversion or gainsaying. Make them in every congregation a savor of life unto life, rejoicing and quickening the hearts of thy people, convincing and converting sinners, and adding to thy Church many of such as shall be saved.

O Lord, we ask thy blessing upon the instruction given this day in Sunday-schools. Let every faithful teacher carry in his own bosom a reward for his labor of love, and come back to it with renewed and enlarged zeal and knowledge and prayerfulness. If any have been unfaithful in their work, show them their delinquency, give them repentance for it, and bring them again to their duty resolved in thy strength to seek the blessing of those whom, being faithful over a few things, thou wilt make rulers over many things. Lord, seal instruction upon the youthful mind. May they acknowledge thy claims upon their hearts, and now, while they are in the dew of their youth, and before the evil days come, may they remember their Creator and serve thee in newness of life.

Gracious God, we beseech thee to grant us they favor in all the things thou seest we need. If we ask amiss, forgive; if we fail to ask, bestow; and let our persons and services be accepted before thee in Jesus our Redeemer. Amen.

READING LIST FOR THE LORD'S DAY

I have listed below suitable reading for the Lord's Day. I have divided the list into three categories: children, youth, and adult. Of course, many other titles could have been included. Where possible, I have given the name of the publisher.

CHILDREN

God's Riches (Workbook on the Doctrines of Grace) (Banner of Truth)
Ferguson, Sinclair. *The Big Book of Questions and Answers* (Christian Focus)
Harding, Susan. *Tell Me About God* (Banner of Truth)
Lindvall, Ella K. *Read-Aloud Bible Stories* Vols. 1-4 (Moody)
Mackenzie, Carine. *Children of the Bible* (Christian Focus)
Mackenzie, *The Life of Jesus* (CFP)
Mackenzie, Carine. *The Caring Creator* (Christian Focus)
Mackenzie, Carine. *The Followers of Jesus* (Christian Focus)
Schoolland, Marian M. *Leading Little Ones to God* (Banner of Truth)
Sproul, R. C. *The King Without a Shadow* (Chariot)
de Vries, Anne. *The Child's Story Bible* (Christian Focus)
Vos, Catherine F. *Children's Story Bible* (Banner of Truth/Eerdmans)
Weber, Rhlannon. *Signposts From Proverbs* (Banner of Truth)

YOUTH

Beeke, James W. *Bible Doctrine for Younger Children, Older Children, Teens and Young Adults*, 7 vol. Set.
Calvin, John. *Biblical Christianity* (Grace Publications)
Hanks, Geoffrey. *70 Great Christians* (Christian Focus)
Henry, Matthew. *The Young Christian* (Christian Focus)
James, John A. *Addresses to Young Men*
James, John A. *Female Piety* (The Young woman's Friend & Guide).
James, John Angel. *Female Piety* (Sol Deo Gloria)
Janeway, James & Mather, Cotton. *A Token for Children* (Sol Deo Gloria)
Lewis, C. S. *The Chronicles of Narnia* (Harper-Collins)
Luther, Martin. *Born Slaves* (Grace Publications)
Pike, J. G. *Persuasives to Early Piety* (Sol Deo Gloria)
Spurgeon, C.H. *A Good Start: A Book for Young Men & Women*. (Sol Deo Gloria)
Tallach, John. *They Shall be Mine* (Banner of Truth)

ADULT

Alexander, Archibald. *Thoughts on Religious Experience*

Barker, William. *Puritan Profiles* (Christian Focus)

Beeke, Gerstner, MacArthur, Sproul, et al. *Justification By Faith Alone* (Sol Deo Gloria)

Bennett, Arthur. *The Valley of Vision* (Banner of Truth)

Bonar, Andrew. *Memoir & Remains of Robert Murray McCheyne* (Banner of Truth)

Bonar, Horatius. *Everlasting Righteousness* (Banner of Truth)

Bonar, Horatius. *God's Way of Holiness.*

Brooks, Thomas. *Heaven on Earth* (Banner of Truth)

Bunyan, John. *Pilgrims' Progress.*

Chantry, Walter. *Call the Sabbath a Delight* (Banner of Truth)

Ferguson, Sinclair. *Discovering God's Will* (Banner of Truth)

Ferguson, Sinclair. *Grow in Grace* (Banner of Truth)

Henry, Matthew. *A Method for Prayer* (Christian Focus).

Horton, Michael. *In the Face of God* (Word)

Knox, John. *The Reformation in Scotland* (Banner of Truth)

Lloyd-Jones, D.M. *The Puritans* (Banner of Truth)

M'Cheyne, Robert M. *A Basket of Fragments* (Christian Focus)

M'Cheyne, Robert M. *From the Preacher's Heart* (Christian Focus)

Murray, Iain. *Jonathan Edwards, A New Biography* (Banner of Truth)

Packer, James I. *A Quest for Godliness: The Puritan Vision of the Christian Life*

Piper, John. *The Pleasures of God* (Multnomah)

Pink, A.W. *Sovereignty of God* (Banner of Truth)

Roberts, Maurice. *The Thought of God* (Banner of Truth)

Rutherford, Samuel. *Letters of Samuel Rutherford.*

Ryle, J.C. *Holiness* (Evangelical Press)

Scougal, Henry. *The Life of God in the Soul of Man* (Christian Focus)

Steele, Richard. *A Remedy for Wandering Thoughts During Worship.* (Sprinkle)

Vander Velde, Frances. *Women of the Bible* (Kregel)

Venning, Ralph. *The Sinfulness of Sin.* (Banner of Truth)

Watson, Thomas. *The Lord's Prayer* (Banner of Truth)

Watson, Thomas. *The Ten Commandments* (Banner of Truth)

Winslow, Octavius. *Personal Declension and Revival of Religion in the Soul* (Banner of Truth)

INDEX OF PERSONS

The letter 'n' indicates a footnote: 'ns' indicates more than one footnote.

INDEX OF SUBJECTS

Italics are used for titles of works and for Greek words (anglicized). The letter 'n' indicates a footnote: 'ns' has been used to indicate more than one footnote.

250

SCRIPTURE INDEX

Bibliography

Beckwith, Roger T. and Wilfrid Stott, *This is the Day* (The Biblical doctrine of the Christian Sunday), The Attic Press, Inc.

Carson, D.A., *From Sabbath to Lord's Day: A Biblical, Historical, and Theological Investigation*, Zondervan, 1982.

Chantry, Walter, *Call the Sabbath A Delight*, The Banner of Truth Trust, 1991.

Dabney, Robert L., 'The Christian Sabbath: Its Nature, Design and Proper Observance' in *Discussions: Evangelical and Theological*, Vol. 1.

Dabney, Robert L., *Lectures in Systematic Theology*, Grand Rapids, Zondervan, 1972.

Edwards, Jonathan, 'The Perpetuity and Change of the Sabbath' in *The Works of Jonathan Edwards*, Vol. II, p. 93.

Fairbairn, Patrick, 'Views of the Reformers Regarding the Sabbath' in *The Typology of Scripture*, vol. II, pp. 447-459. Zondervan reprint, n.d.

Hodge, Archibald A., *The Day Changed and the Sabbath Preserved*, Philadelphia: Great Commission Publications, n.d.

Hodge, Charles, *Systematic Theology*, 3 vols, Grand Rapids, Eerdmans, 1975.

Hoeksema, Herman, 'The Idea of the Sabbath' in *The Triple Knowledge* (Expositions on the Heidelberg Catechism), Vol. III, Reformed Free Publishing Association.

Jewett, Paul K., *The Lord's Day: A Theological Guide to the Christian Day of Worship*, Eerdmans, 1971.

Murray, John. 'The Moral Law and the Fourth Commandment' in *Collected Writings of John Murray*, vol. I, pp. 193-228. The Banner of Truth Trust, 1976.

Murray, John, *Principles of Conduct*, Grand Rapids, Eerdmans, 1964.

Owen, John, 'The Name, Original Nature, Use and Continuance of a Day of Sacred Rest' in *The Works of John Owen*, Vol. 19.

Massenlink, William, 'Meaning and Observance of the Sabbath' in *Sermons on the Ten Commandments* (by ministers of the Reformed and Christian Reformed Churches) edited by Henry J. Kuiper, Zondervan.

Rayburn, Robert G, *Should Christians Observe the Sabbath?* Presbyterian, vol. 10, pp 72-86. n.p. 1984.

Shephard, Thomas, *Theses Sabbaticae*, vol. 3 of works, Ligonier, (PA), 1992.

Warfield, B.B., 'The Foundations of the Sabbath in the Word of God' in *Selected Short Writings of B. B. Warfield*, Vol. II, Presbyterian and Reformed Publishing Company.